THROUGH HIS EYES

Through HIS EYES

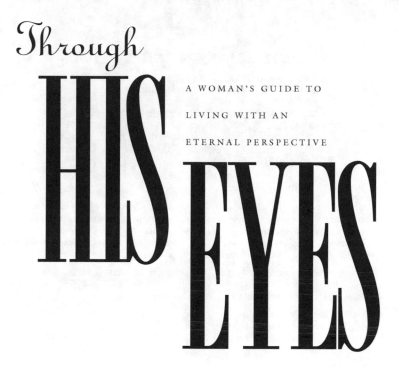

A WOMAN'S GUIDE TO
LIVING WITH AN
ETERNAL PERSPECTIVE

KATHY COLLARD MILLER

NAVPRESS

BRINGING TRUTH TO LIFE

P.O. Box 35001, Colorado Springs, Colorado 80935

OUR GUARANTEE TO YOU

We believe so strongly in the message of our books that we are making this quality guarantee to you. If for any reason you are disappointed with the content of this book, return the title page to us with your name and address and we will refund to you the list price of the book. To help us serve you better, please briefly describe why you were disappointed. Mail your refund request to: NavPress, P.O. Box 35002, Colorado Springs, CO 80935.

The Navigators is an international Christian organization. Our mission is to reach, disciple, and equip people to know Christ and to make Him known through successive generations. We envision multitudes of diverse people in the United States and every other nation who have a passionate love for Christ, live a lifestyle of sharing Christ's love, and multiply spiritual laborers among those without Christ.

NavPress is the publishing ministry of The Navigators. NavPress publications help believers learn biblical truth and apply what they learn to their lives and ministries. Our mission is to stimulate spiritual formation among our readers.

ISBN 1-57683-117-5

Cover photo by Sara Gray/ Tony Stone Images
Cover design by Dan Jamison
Creative Team: Traci Mullins, Casandra Lindell, Terry Behimer, Lori Mitchell, Tim Howard

Some of the anecdotal illustrations in this book are true to life and are included with the permission of the persons involved. All other illustrations are composites of real situations, and any resemblance to people living or dead is coincidental.

Unless otherwise identified, all Scripture quotations in this publication are taken from the *New American Standard Bible* (NASB), © The Lockman Foundation 1960, 1962, 1963, 1968, 1971, 1972, 1973, 1975, 1977. Other versions used include: THE *HOLY BIBLE: NEW INTERNATIONAL VERSION* ® (NIV®). Copyright © 1973, 1978, 1984 by International Bible Society, used by permission of Zondervan Publishing House, all rights reserved; the *Revised Standard Version Bible* (RSV), copyright 1946, 1952, 1971, by the Division of Christian Education of the National Council of the Churches of Christ in the USA, used by permission, all rights reserved; *The Living Bible* (TLB), copyright © 1971, used by permission of Tyndale House Publishers, Inc., Wheaton, IL 60189, all rights reserved and *The New Testament in Modern English* (PH), J. B. Phillips Translator, © J. B. Phillips 1958, 1960, 1972, used by permission of Macmillan Publishing Company.

Printed in the United States of America

1 2 3 4 5 6 7 8 9 10 11 12 13 14 15 / 05 04 03 02 01 00 99

FOR A FREE CATALOG OF
NAVPRESS BOOKS & BIBLE STUDIES,
CALL 1-800-366-7788 (USA)
OR 1-416-499-4615 (CANADA)

I'm grateful to dear friends

Joyce Williams
Cheryl Teichert
Pat LaGraffe
Kim Ocheltree
Brenda Glasby

who impact my life with
fun, accountability, support, and encouragement,
and who help me see life through God's eyes.

Contents

Acknowledgments

I'm deeply grateful to many people who have supported me and encouraged me in the writing of this book. When I faced a challenge during some rewriting, I put out a "HELP!" call and some great friends came to my rescue with insights and anecdotes. Thanks to Dianne Janak, Bonnie Jeffers, Karen Dye, Melanie Hubbard, Diane Bechtle, Sue Mellis, Ruthie Swain, Sue VanLant, Judy Prince, and Jennifer Botkin Phillips. You're the greatest!

Through His Eyes would not have become the book it is without the wise analysis of NavPress editorial director Sue Geiman and the expert editing—along with encouraging direction—of Traci Mullins of Eclipse Editorial Services. I'm deeply grateful for your input and support.

I can never thank my prayer partners enough for lifting me up before God's throne as I work through each project. Your prayers make a difference. And for the members of our family Bible study, who often hear me express my stress, thanks for listening and praying. Mother, Leslie, Dorie, and Debbie, I enjoy our times together.

I could never do what I do without my husband Larry's incredible support and encouragement. He serves me and spurs me on to serve God. Honey, thanks for everything you do for me and how you empower me with your love, humor, trust, and blessings.

Darcy and Mark, you're the greatest children in the world. I'm proud of you both and love you to pieces. Thanks for how God uses you to help me look at life and people through God's eyes.

Heavenly Father, I desire for you to receive the acknowledgment and glory through this book. Thank You for the privilege of serving a great God like You.

1

Looking at Life
Through the Lens of
Eternity

Heaven invites you to set the lens of your heart on
the heart of the Savior and make Him the object of
your life.

MAX LUCADO

[The heaven-minded Christian] walks by a simple and
pure faith, . . . and when this sojourner looks out of his
own eyes, he sees things as though he were looking
through the eyes of God.

He sees his own life, he sees his surrounding circumstances, he sees the other believers, he sees friends and
enemies, he sees principalities and powers, he sees the
whole course of the pageantry of history itself through
the eyes of God . . . and is content.

MADAME JEANNE GUYON

*M*Y HOME IS LESS THAN A MILE AWAY FROM A LAKE—AS THE ducks fly. About this time every year we have some of the ducks who reside there decide their old home isn't a good enough place for the birth of their ducklings. They come and check out our swimming pool.

Yesterday I chased a future mom and dad duck away from our pool and they were disgruntled about it. As I approached, they quacked a little and as I closed in, they quacked louder, finally succumbing to the persistent flapping of my wings, er, arms.

I tried to tell them, "Your babies won't do well here. There isn't any of the food they need and the chlorinated pool water isn't good for you all. Besides, you'll make a mess around here and then I'll be disgruntled!"

They didn't seem convinced by my logic because I had to chase them away several times throughout the day. I suppose I'll have to continue that process tomorrow since they aren't looking at this situation from my perspective at all. But in this situation I know best: The lake is a better place.

My ducky experience reminds me of my relationship with God. Just like those ducks, I go looking for something I think will meet my needs that God advises against. I'm convinced I know best when He actually does.

More than ten years ago, I became intrigued with the idea that God sees the whole picture. I began trying to live according to the truth: "God loves me and wants the best for me. If I can just see life from His perspective, I may be able to understand it better and live the abundant life He promises."

I realized there was a difference between my earthly perspective and His heavenly one. When I keep my eyes focused on earthly values, I'm disgruntled, angry, disillusioned, and critical. I can only view my life from a limited plane, but He can see everything, both now and in the future. Why shouldn't I desire such a better viewpoint? I'm convinced that when I do see life through God's eyes, my faith flourishes and I can respond in a godly way.

Having a heavenly viewpoint of this earthly walk is really where we desire to live. But sometimes our need to find satisfaction in this world overrides our ability to look at life from God's perspective. We become angry, tense, self-focused. Someone has defined sin as trying to get a need met in a way God never intended. An earthly mindset is, basically, trying to get a particular legitimate need met through a self-centered way that isn't part of God's plan. But God designed us and created us. He always knows what's best!

A New Pair of Glasses

In contrast, society communicates an earthly philosophy of, "You can meet your own needs." It tells us we can "do it all," like Superwomen. Such unrealistic expectations focus on the accomplishments of the here and now, not dependence upon God and the value of spiritual growth.

The world is seeking anything that can fill up the God-shaped vacuum inside the human soul. People do it with a variety of things. When the trailer for the new *Star Wars* movie, *The Phantom Menace*, previewed, the response of people was very interesting. Now, I'm a huge fan of *Star Wars*, but we're talking here about the *trailer!* You know, that thirty-second to two-minute advertisement about a coming movie. Evidently, the trailer was hyped at theaters and people paid to see just the two-minute promotion film—a sneak preview of a preview! These people paid full price for admittance to a regular movie, knowing the trailer would be shown at the beginning. And then many of them left after the trailer was aired . . . before the scheduled movie.

One man said, as he exited, that he would have paid fifty dollars to see the trailer. He continued, "I've been waiting so long for this, I cried. This just restores my faith in mankind!"

Talk about an earthly perspective of getting our needs met!

In order to move toward a heavenly viewpoint, we need to ask ourselves questions like:

- "Am I looking for something to meet my needs that God never intended to be able to do that?"
- "Does God want me to take on a responsibility? Do I want to say "yes" because I don't want anyone to think I can't handle it?"
- "Am I trying to feel loved through people's approval or by knowing God loves me regardless of my performance?"
- "How can I release my bitterness about being rejected when it feels good to nurse my hurt?"
- "If I trust God to change that person, will I accept His way of doing that?"

I know I struggle in those areas. I want to focus on the "here and now" rather than on what God wants to do in and through me so that I'll have treasures stored up in heaven. I focus on "needing" that dress at the department store sale rather than dressing my soul with luxurious garments of praise. I feel compelled to help people see how talented I am rather than magnify my Lord and Savior, who provided those talents and gifts.

Other women have shared with me that their spiritual eyes get bloodshot when a friend misunderstands something they say and breaks off a friendship. They feel like a failure instead of trusting God to restore the relationship. They also indicate that worry is one of the strongest things that makes their spiritual vision blur.

When you and I have eye problems such as bloodshot eyes, we can bathe our eyes with a soothing product created for that. If we have nearsightedness or farsightedness, we get fitted for glasses or contact lenses. Or we might even consider corrective surgery. Similarly, when we have spiritual eyesight problems, we need to take steps to correct our blurred vision. I like to think of that as putting on spiritual glasses. These spiritual glasses represent Jesus' view of life.

In this book we will explore several common earthly perspectives that can blur our spiritual vision, and we'll consider the biblical viewpoints we need to develop in order to correct our outlook. The chart below outlines the earthly perspective each chapter addresses, along with the "corrective lens" an eternal perspective provides.

Chapter	Earthly Perspective	Eternal Perspective
Grace	I have to perform in order to be loved.	Because of God's grace, I am loved unconditionally.
Identity	My accomplishments define who I am.	I am a child of God and I have an inheritance in Christ.
Faith	Suffering should be avoided at all costs.	God uses my problems to refine me and draw me closer to Him.
Purpose	Life can't be enjoyed unless it's "good."	My purpose is to glorify God whether or not my life conforms to the world's definition of "good."
Service	I must take care of myself because nobody else will.	I can be a living sacrifice because God will take care of me.
Humility	I have every right to be proud.	I can choose humility and boast in the Lord.
Forgiveness	I want to focus on the past and punish those who hurt me.	I can forgive what is past and look forward to the future.
Surrender	I need to control others.	I will let God change others as I influence them.
Contentment	I can't be content.	I can choose to be content regardless of circumstances.
Transcendence	I should be comfortable and fulfilled here on earth.	I am a citizen of heaven and I won't be complete until I am at home with God.

As we face life's challenges and practice putting on our spiritual glasses, we'll become more familiar with God's view of our life here on earth. For instance, if my husband, Larry, forgets my birthday, my natural reaction is to be hurt and angry. But if I look through Jesus' glasses at Larry, I'm able to respond to him in a godly manner. That's different from when I don't see him through the "spiritual lens" of Jesus' perspective. Through heavenly vision, I'm able to see Larry as a child of God, loved by Jesus. God wants me to love him unconditionally. If I view Larry through my spiritual glasses when he does something that angers me, I can quiet my frustration and communicate in a loving way.

Seeing through God's lenses will enable us to behave within a godly framework. As a result, we'll lay up for ourselves eternal rewards and reap abundant benefits here on earth. We'll experience the wonderful fruit of the Spirit that Galatians 5:22-23 tells us about: love, joy, peace, patience, kindness, goodness, faithfulness, gentleness, and self-control.

Our future destination is guaranteed. But our present ability to live a fulfilling and godly life becomes more of a reality by cultivating an eternal perspective. That's a winning proposition.

Opening Our Spiritual Eyes

As we examine different earthly perspectives in the chapters ahead and then replace those perspectives with the appropriate eternal viewpoint, our spiritual eyes will be opened. This can be likened to what happened to Elisha's servant in 2 Kings 6:8-17. Elisha, the servant of God, had warned the king of Israel of the plans of Israel's enemies. As a result, the enemy king sent his army to capture Elisha at the town of Dothan. Elisha's servant looked over the wall and saw all the soldiers, horses, and chariots. As any of us would be, he was afraid and cried out, "Master! Look at all those soldiers! We're doomed! There's no way you and I can fight them all. And this city can't hold out against them."

Elisha answers, "Don't be afraid, because there are many more on our side than on theirs."

Now at this point, the servant most likely rolled his eyes in disgust and disbelief. He probably looked around and didn't see anyone standing up for them. Maybe the townsfolk were even willing to hand Elisha over to the enemy to avoid a battle that could destroy their town. The servant must have been thinking, "Oh, sure, we've only got a few of these townspeople who don't even know how to fight or don't have weapons. We really are dead meat!"

But then he hears Elisha pray, "O LORD, open his eyes that he may see." And in that moment, as the servant looks out over the hills beyond Dothan, he suddenly sees the mountain full of horses and chariots of fire standing ready to protect the man of God. "Hey," he might have cried out, "where did all that great army come from? Did they just arrive?"

No, they were there all along, but his spiritual eyes hadn't seen the army of God before. He had been looking only with earthly, fearful eyes at the enemy. Through Elisha's prayer and God opening his eyes, he became aware of God's protection. He needed to see his surroundings with spiritual eyes, not physical eyes.

In a like manner, our spiritual eyes can be blinded by a temporal frame of mind. But just as Elisha's servant's eyes were opened at that dusty town of Dothan, the eyes of our spirit can be opened. Then we'll suddenly see that God is more powerful and wise than we realized. He is providing everything we need.

In our next chapter, we'll discover how to have our spiritual eyes opened so we can know the truth about God's unconditional grace when we start to think we must perform in order to be loved by Him. But first, I've got to tend to the ducks. They're splashing around in our pool again. I can't communicate to the ducks that want to live in my backyard that they're better off at the park, but I'm glad God can communicate with us regardless of our spiritual myopia. If we are willing to look in His direction, He will correct our vision and prepare us for eternity with Him.

Grace

*Because of God's grace,
I am loved unconditionally.*

There is no need to plead that the love of God shall fill our heart as though he were unwilling to fill us. He is willing as light is willing to flood a room that is opened to its brightness.

AMY CARMICHAEL

Every time the thought of grace appears, there is the idea of its being undeserved. In no way is the recipient getting what he or she deserves. Favor is being extended simply out of the goodness of the heart of the giver.

CHARLES SWINDOLL

*A*S A CHILD, I BELIEVED I NEEDED TO PERFORM PERFECTLY IN ORDER to earn God's love and approval, along with the approval of other people in my life. Because I was born in a "Christian" nation and attended church faithfully, I believed I was a Christian. Yet, I still felt uneasy because I never fully sensed that God loved me. I envisioned Him standing up in heaven, His arms crossed at His chest, tapping His toe and muttering, "Kathy, when are you going to become perfect so I can love you?"

I read the Bible and in it God said, "Become perfect as I am perfect." The burden of becoming perfect was so heavy that, at the age of thirteen, I took a symbolic bubble bath at the stroke of midnight on New Year's Eve. As I enjoyed the warm, cleansing bubbles, I prayed, "God, please forgive me for everything I've done wrong and I vow to You to never do anything wrong for the rest of my life." I figured a sinless performance would be sufficient to guarantee my entrance into heaven when I died and give me the ability to sense God's approval while living on earth.

When I couldn't become perfect because—horrors!—I did something wrong the very next day, I still felt compelled to add something to God's grace. I began to keep track of my deeds on an imaginary scale. On one side of the scale, I stacked my good deeds, and on the other, my bad deeds. I concluded, "Certainly I'll have more good deeds than bad deeds by the time I die. Then God will have to approve of me and let me into heaven because I've been such a good girl." Because I couldn't place anything on the good side of the scale unless it was done perfectly, I constantly felt burdened by the weighted-down bad side of the scale. *When am I going to become good enough?* I constantly wondered.

It wasn't until several years later, at the age of eighteen, that the truth of God's wonderful grace broke through my earthly perspective. I began dating Larry in our senior year of high school. Several months later, I attended his church, where I heard clearly for the first time about God's unconditional love and grace—a grace that offered salvation as a free gift, nothing additional needed, not even my good works. With relief and joy, I asked Jesus to come into my life and become my Lord and Savior on that Sunday morning, October 1, 1967. The image of the scale was thrown away and I began to understand grace.

Of course, that didn't take away all my tendencies to perform for God's approval. It has been a continuing process of putting on spiritual glasses that confirm God offers me gracious love instead of requiring me to earn His acceptance.

My friend, Diane, has been through a similar process. In the past, her performance tendencies were revealed through an eating disorder. She explained, "I believed the image of what others mirrored to me. I had to uphold an image of being a perfect wife and mother, having a perfect shape, and having perfect children. As I've learned and experienced God's grace through His unconditional love for me, I can now relax a little and extend grace to others. I'm learning who I really am—my strengths and weaknesses—and I'm beginning to be able to work within the realm of my personality and giftedness instead of being all things to all people."

Diane is wearing the glasses that reveal how God's wonderful grace is more important than the approval of people. As a result, she is enjoying the benefit of loving herself and others more unconditionally.

Many other women report that their desire to perform is expressed in varying ways. One woman shared with me, "Succeeding in my job was essential because my father raised me to think I can do anything. He valued job performance. He rarely gave me affection, but when I got good grades in the classes he considered important, he would give me a big hug."

Another woman told me that when she wanted to talk to her mother, her babysitter told her, "Your mother is busy doing something important. She can't talk to you right now." As a result, she felt unimportant and was always trying to get her mother's attention through her drawing and painting—something her mother valued.

There can be many underlying causes for our desire to perform—for God's approval and the approval of others. But as we begin to understand God's unconditional love, our need for people's approval often diminishes. After all, if the Almighty God of the Universe Who knows all of our faults and inner needs accepts us, then the approval of people can become less essential.

Amazing Grace!

Grace truly is amazing! Author Philip Yancey tells about a British conference where experts from all over the world gathered to discuss comparative religions. They began trying to decide on the one belief unique to Christians. He writes, "They began eliminating possibilities. Incarnation? Other religions had different versions of gods appearing in human form. Resurrection? Again, other religions had accounts of return from death. The debate went on for some time until C. S. Lewis wandered into the room. 'What's the rumpus about?' he asked, and heard in reply that his colleagues were discussing Christianity's unique contribution among world religions. In his forthright manner Lewis responded, 'Oh, that's easy. It's grace.'

"After some discussion, the conferees had to agree. The notion of God's love coming to us free of charge, no strings attached, seems to go against every instinct of humanity. The Buddhist eightfold path, the Hindu doctrine of karma, the Jewish covenant, and the Muslim code of law—each of these offers a way to earn approval. Only Christianity dares to make God's love unconditional."[1]

The world offers a way to earn approval, but God offers His approval as a free gift. Grace is that undeserved love and favor God offers us, even though He knows we can never deserve it, earn it, or repay Him for it. Titus 3:5 assures us, "He saved us, not on the basis of deeds which we have done in righteousness, but according to His mercy, by the washing of regeneration and renewing by the Holy Spirit."

That kind of unconditional love was demonstrated for me many years ago when Larry and I attended the wedding of our friends, Rick and Fausta. Larry and Rick were both policemen at the same department and I had just recently met Fausta. When it was time to leave after the sit-down dinner, Larry and I went up to the newly-weds. "We wish you the very best," Larry said, shaking Rick's hand and giving Fausta a peck on the cheek.

I grinned and said, "The wedding was gorgeous and the reception was incredible. Thank you for a wonderful time."

Rick and Fausta accepted our greetings with a smile. Then Fausta said, "Kathy, wait just a moment. I have a gift for you."

Fausta turned and walked away. I stood there dumbfounded. *Wait a minute,* I thought. *I brought Fausta a gift. She's not supposed to give me a gift. I'm not in her wedding so I didn't earn a gift and I didn't do anything to help her—so I don't deserve anything. We only met recently. Why is she giving me a gift?* I was amazed! I turned to Larry with a questioning look, but he returned my gaze as if to say, "Don't look at me. I don't know what's going on."

Within moments, Fausta returned. In her hand she carried a white box four or five inches square with a delicate white ribbon wrapped around it. As she offered me the gift, I wanted to say, "Fausta, I can't take this from you. I brought you a gift; you're not supposed to give me a gift. It's your wedding, not mine!" But realizing how rude that would be, I instead reached out my hand, took the box, and said, "Fausta, that's so sweet of you. Thank you very much."

As we drove home, I began to untie the ribbon. Inside, a small seal read, "Made in Milan, Italy." I gasped. "Oh, Larry. This must be expensive. It says it's made in Italy. Why did she give me this gift?"

I quickly pulled the box top off, peeled away the layer of tissue paper, and stared at a beautiful, sterling silver candy dish.

"Look, Larry. Isn't it lovely?" Larry nodded as I turned it over and over, studying its beauty. Then I noticed engraving in the center of the dish. "Larry, the letters R and F are engraved in the center, to remind me they gave it to me."

Then a wonderful thought dawned on me. "Larry, this dish could symbolize the gift of salvation God gave you and me. Just as I didn't do anything to deserve or earn this dish, so God offered the gift of His love and of being His child, even though I couldn't do anything to earn or deserve it. Isn't that just like His grace? And since Fausta hardly knows me, it represents God's generosity."

Larry's smile confirmed he knew exactly what I was talking about, especially since he was the one who had introduced me to God's gift so many years earlier.

I still don't know why Rick and Fausta gave me that beautiful gift. I have to believe that it was a custom of Fausta's family's native Italy that everyone at the wedding received a similar gift. That silver dish gently reminds me of God's wonderful gift of grace, something I never could have been good enough to earn or deserve. And I'm also reminded that just as those initials "R F" are engraved into that dish, the Holy Spirit has engraved His initials into my soul. I belong to God because I'm "marked" and "sealed" by God's Spirit.

Ephesians 1:13-14 affirms, " . . . having also believed, you were sealed in Him with the Holy Spirit of promise, who is given as a pledge of our inheritance. . . ." The "seal" Paul refers to is like our modern-day notary stamp. It authenticates and makes the document valid, thus holding accountable the people who sign the document. In a like manner, God is saying, "I'm pledging Myself to always consider you My child, no matter what. Here's My mark of My Spirit to demonstrate My commitment."

There is a significant difference between God's mark on my soul and the engraving on the candy dish: Someone may somehow be able to scrape the initials off my candy dish, but the seal God has placed in my spirit cannot be removed. If it could, God's gift would be based on my performance and not His grace.

It has also occurred to me that if Rick and Fausta intended everyone to have a similar gift, some of the guests may have left the reception without giving their verbal best wishes and thanks to the newlyweds. If so, they may not have received their beautiful gift, just as those who don't approach God don't receive His gift of grace. God's grace is intended for everyone. Jesus died on the cross for each and every one of us. God loves the whole world, but unless we each come to Him to say, "Thanks for dying for me," we won't receive His gracious gift of love and eternal life.

Modern-Day Prodigal Daughter

That gracious gift is best illustrated through Jesus' story about the prodigal son in Luke 15. You may remember the story of the son who chooses to leave his family behind, take his inheritance, and live apart from his loving father. But his selfishness causes him to squander all his money on high living and immorality. He ends up eating the refuse intended for the pigs.

In a moment of clarity and honesty, he realizes his sin and returns to his family, intending to become a servant in his father's household. But the father has been longing to restore him and daily looks out his window wanting to see his beloved son return. When the father finally sees his son's form walking down the dusty street, his shoulders hunched over in defeat and despair, the forgiving father runs to him, kisses him, and restores him to his rightful place as a *son*, not just a servant. What glorious grace! Grace that forgives and forgets as only God can do.

Kay Arthur, founder of Precept Ministries, is a self-proclaimed modern-day prodigal daughter who experienced the Father's gracious love and forgiveness after straying far from Him. When first married, she and her husband called themselves Christians and "played church." But life was very difficult because Kay's husband experienced periods of deep depression. She says that her self-centeredness caused her to leave him with their children. But because she craved the security of being loved, she went from one man to another. As she says, "In the process, I became something

I never wanted, never dreamed I would ever be. I became an adulteress. Yet all I wanted was security."

Her search for intimacy and security ended at age twenty-nine when she knelt and called out to God. He became her El Shaddai, her "All-sufficient One." Though she had reached the low level of immorality, when she turned and walked back toward God with her shoulders hunched over in defeat and despair, God ran toward her with His arms outstretched and whispered, "Beloved daughter, you're back! I'm so glad. I want to meet all your needs and take care of everything that concerns you. Welcome!"

Just as the prodigal son tried to refuse his father's love, Kay may not have felt worthy of that gracious acceptance. But God proved His love through the years ahead as He strengthened her during her first husband's suicide and her struggle as a single parent raising two sons. Eventually, He called her into a ministry of encouraging others to seek God through His Word.[2]

Whether or not your own struggle has reached the depths the prodigal son or Kay Arthur experienced, we all have turned our backs on God to some degree. But as soon as we turn around and run toward Him, He opens His arms and welcomes us back without condemnation or required performance. He's just thrilled that we want to be welcomed back into His family.

A Missing Obstacle

Another wrong view of God's grace is depicted well by what happened to me some time ago as I arrived at a local regional park to have my monthly morning in prayer. I was pleased with my organization: I was even prepared with the six quarters I needed to enter the park. Driving up to the automatic gate, I put my six quarters into the slot and turned my gaze forward expecting to see the automatic arm ascending. What I hadn't noticed before, though, was that the automatic arm that usually blocked the way wasn't there at all.

Where is it? I muttered to myself. *Oh, it must be broken.* Then

I realized, *I didn't have to put in my money! I could have gone in for free!*

Later, as I sat in the park reading my Bible and relaxing in God's presence, I thought about that incident. I realized that's how I often approach God. I put in my quarter of "Lord, I had my devotions. Do you love me now?" or "Lord, here's my quarter of loving that person I hate. Do you accept me now?" I try to earn God's favor and love along with His acceptance by doing the right thing, hoping my good behavior will impress Him so He'll be pleased with my devotion.

Looking at life through the lens of eternity empowers us to recognize that the mechanical arm separating us from His love and favor is no longer there! We aren't prevented from "driving" into His unconditional love and acceptance by anything because Jesus' death and resurrection closed the gulf between us and God. As a result, we can rejoice that there's nothing we can do to make God love us more, and there's nothing we can do to make God love us less.

That's the kind of unconditional love that my friend Dianne experienced as a twelve-year-old. For the first time, she felt loved while attending a six-week Christian girls' camp in Texas. She had left behind a horrible family life of an alcoholic father and verbally abusive mother. From the time she was three years old, her mother told her that Dianne was the worst mistake of her life. Daily, her mother said she wished her daughter had never been born. Dianne tried desperately and persistently to win her mother's favor and love, but her excellent grades and overachieving efforts at school never gained her the love and acceptance she desired from a cold and cruel mother.

But when she attended that Christian camp, Dianne felt something new. She didn't know what it was at the time but now she knows it was God's love. For the first time, she felt as if she belonged and that people cared about her. She felt safe. For those six weeks, she didn't hear her parents fighting and her mother berating her. She laughed and played and excelled in the sports program. She made new friends who accepted her as a loved and valued person. And she loved them too.

On the last night of the camp, as the campfire blazed, the three hundred girls were in tears with their arms around each other as they sang their familiar camp songs about God, love, and friendship. Their parents all sat in rows of chairs behind them. Dianne hoped her mother could feel what was bursting inside of her. She hoped that by just being there, her mother would know that there could be joy and peace because of God's love.

The awards were being given out for the best swimmer, best horseback rider, best cabin, best counselor, and other achievements. But the most important award was saved for last: "Best Camper." This coveted award was voted on by all the campers and counselors and had never in the seventy-five-year history of the camp been awarded to a first-year camper. Even though Dianne's name was on the ballot, she knew she had no chance of winning because this was her first time at the camp.

But then her name was called as the winner. Dianne remembers, "I thought, 'How odd . . . someone else has my name.' Suddenly thirty girls were surrounding me, crying and trying to hug me as they pushed me up to the front to receive my award. I remember feeling something that night that I know now was God Himself reaching down from heaven, saying . . . 'I am well pleased and you are accepted. . . .' The people around me didn't really seem to matter at that moment. The cup I held in my hand was itself just a symbol. What really mattered was that my heart was filled to overflowing with the awesome beauty of God's love for me. I knew in that instance that He truly had a purpose for my life."

Dianne continues, "I looked in the crowd for my mother. I knew that this was my moment of truth, and finally now she would approve of me. She would hug me and smile and say how proud she was of me. She would be sorry for all those things she had said to me over the years and we would go home to become the family I'd always longed to have. I believed with all my heart that God had finally let me achieve something good to win her affection, her approval, and her love. I knew that my life would finally be what

I imagined life was for all my friends but had somehow eluded me."

When Dianne found her mother, her heart was pounding with excitement. But her mother was staring at the ground with a frown on her face. Then she looked at Dianne and said, "How did you deserve something like that?"

In that cruel moment, Dianne's joy was stolen and she again slipped back into her old way of thinking. Her mother's words had confirmed her greatest fears: She didn't deserve God's love and could never find the approval and acceptance she craved, from her mother or from God.

Though her heart had broken within her, she still had a small token of the joy of that camp: the trophy! For two weeks she enjoyed it. When life got bleak and painful, the trophy reminded her that God had reached down from heaven and touched her heart.

But after two weeks, the trophy disappeared. Her mother, in a fit of disapproval, removed it and never returned it. Dianne couldn't ask about it for she knew it would only bring more hatred and disapproval.

Many years later, after finding Christ as her personal Savior at age twenty-nine, getting married, and having a family, the thought of her mother's hurtful words still haunted her. As God began the healing process in her life, Dianne shared that destructive childhood scene with a friend. That friend encouraged her to buy a trophy, put her maiden name on it with the date of the camp, and allow herself to experience God's love again in a tangible way. Though she felt silly, Dianne did it, and the trophy sits in her home, a reminder of God's touch of grace and love when she believed she could never deserve or earn His love. God had reached down into the life of an abused child and showered His unconditional favor and acceptance during a six-week period of her life. That favor was represented by a trophy that could be removed, but God's love can never be stolen or removed by anyone.

We all sometimes feel that the "trophy" of God's love and acceptance has been stolen because we didn't perform well or weren't good enough. But we can learn to see through God's eyes that it can't be removed. Satan will try to steal it by telling you that you must be good enough to earn God's love. Other people may try to remove it from the mantel of your heart through mean words, disapproval, or unrealistic expectations. But God offers His gracious love unconditionally, without strings or requirements. The only thing needed is for you to ask Jesus to come into your life to save you from your sins. Grace means you enjoy God's love based on Jesus' sacrifice on the cross, not on your performance.

Earlier I referred to Ephesians 1:13-14 where the apostle Paul wrote that the Holy Spirit seals us as God's children. Those verses also refer to the Holy Spirit as a "pledge" given us by God. The *New International Version* uses the word "deposit," another word for pledge. In a way, that pledge or deposit can be pictured as the trophy Dianne received. Engraved on the trophy's name plate is: "I am loved and accepted by God because of Jesus' death and resurrection." In that sense the Holy Spirit is a "trophy" in our lives representing God's forever, gracious love.

Can you picture that trophy of grace with your name on it? Changing your earthly perspective from "I have to perform in order to be loved" to "God offers unconditional love and grace" will lay a firm foundation for seeing life from God's perspective. Don't let anyone—Satan or another person—steal the trophy of God's unconditional love and grace from the mantel of your heart. Your name can never be removed from that trophy because you are sealed with the Holy Spirit. Keep telling yourself the truth: "I am loved by God and His acceptance has nothing to do with earning or deserving it. It's a free gift because of Jesus' sacrificial death on the cross." That is looking at yourself through God's eyes.

In our next chapter, we'll discover how to view life from God's perspective, even when we're facing trials and dealing with problems. Isn't that the hardest time of all? We'll identify the attitudes we need in order to rise above our circumstances no matter how difficult they are.

❖ *Questions* ❖

1. How do you define "grace?" Feel free to check in the dictionary or a Bible dictionary.

2. Reread on page 22 about the different things the religions of the world offer, as opposed to God's offer of unconditional love through Jesus. How would you explain those differences to a friend who is trying to gain God's approval through one of those religions?

3. In the past, how have you tried to:

   - deserve God's love?

   - earn God's love?

   - repay God for His love?

4. What have your efforts brought you?

5. How is your thinking different after considering God's undeserved grace?

6. Read and meditate on Ephesians 1:13-14. What is:

 ▪ surprising?

 ▪ an important promise?

 ▪ a valuable concept?

 ▪ most meaningful to you?

7. In what ways, big or small, have you been like a prodigal daughter?

8. If you feel separated from God like a prodigal daughter, imagine running up to your heavenly Father and seeing Him fling His arms wide in acceptance and love. Write about your feelings and thoughts after picturing that.

3

Identity

*I am a child of God
and I have an inheritance in Christ.*

With Christ we have everything, without him, nothing
we do, however spectacular, has meaning. Now I know
again what I must rediscover every day: Christ must be
all or he is nothing at all.

Lloyd John Ogilvie

The problem is that human achievement results in
earthly rewards, which fuels the fire for more achievement leading to greater rewards. . . . None of that results
in deep-down satisfaction, an inner peace, a soul-level
contentment, or lasting joy.

Charles Swindoll

*I*F SOMEONE WERE TO ASK, "WHO ARE YOU?" MOST OF US WOULD reply by describing our roles in life—mother, secretary, doctor, wife. In other words, we would explain what we *do*. I hope, however, that none of us would express an attitude like Greta Garbo's. That woman of the big screen died in 1990 at the age of eighty-four. She once said, "My legend is everything to me now. . . . As a matter of fact, I would even sacrifice my own life so as not to jeopardize it." She was a person who found her identity in her achievements and the image she had carefully fostered. To the question, "Who are you?" she might have answered, "My legend."

That's extreme, but I wonder how the man interviewed in an article I read recently would answer that question. I think he might say, "I'm a successful businessman as a result of hard work." In the beginning of the interview, this man asserted that his life was balanced. But when the interviewer asked him about how to become successful, he said that there were no successful people working only forty hours a week. He said they must work longer and harder than the average person. He went on to explain that most millionaires work an average of fifty-nine hours a week. He suggested that people work ten hours five to six days a week.

I found some discrepancies in his philosophy. Although the forty-hour week may no longer be the recipe for even maintaining a job, his overall point seemed to be that work is the most important thing in life. He concluded by saying that happiness is achieved when your deficient needs are finally being satisfied. This man represented the earthly perspective that most people have: Their success or lack of success seems to define them.

Unfortunately, we Christians don't always resist that viewpoint.

Author John Ortberg writes about many pastors who feel hurried, overloaded, drained, and often taken for granted. He describes how he talked with a friend whose father has ministered in Christian circles for close to fifty years. His dad said to him recently, "Well, son, we'll have to get together soon, as soon as I can get my schedule under control."

His son commented: "For all thirty-nine years of my life, my dad has talked about what we're going to do as soon as he gets his schedule under control. He actually seems to believe that someday his schedule will come under control. He refuses to talk about or even acknowledge the real reason why his schedule is out of control."[1]

That pastor seems to believe that his Christian-based activities are more important than his family. Even in doing "God's work" he is ruled by his schedule.

If you and I believe, "My identity is determined by how busy I am," or "My activities reflect my importance" or "I can't stand to do nothing because then I feel insignificant," we are living with an earthly perspective. That's not what God wants for us. Although He is always wanting us to represent Him in the activities He plans for us, He wants us to believe we are valuable and important just because we are His creation and a part of His forever family.

No Confidence in Accomplishments

The apostle Paul came to that same conclusion. After experiencing the ultimate in accomplishments, he came to know Christ personally. Suddenly, all of his incredible deeds and activities seemed totally insignificant. In Philippians 3:4-6, he recounts a long list of things he was given through his human inheritance and through self-effort. He concludes, "But whatever was to my profit I now consider loss for the sake of Christ. What is more, I consider everything a loss compared to the surpassing greatness of knowing Christ Jesus my Lord, for whose sake

I have lost all things. I consider them rubbish, that I may gain Christ" (verses 7-8).

Paul says that if anyone has the right to claim success and consider himself important to his society, it is he! He did it all correctly. His parents gave him the perfect pedigree and his own deeds were impeccable! It might be like someone saying, "I was born into a family that can trace their ancestors back to the Pilgrims. My family has always been loyal to America, and I have ancestors who signed every major document forming the United States. In addition, they were senators and congressmen. And I myself have kept the United States laws from my youth. In fact, I've been a policeman and I'm now a state prosecutor. I make sure other people keep the rules and I prosecute those who don't. Everyone says I'm the toughest attorney around. I pride myself in that I've never broken a law. I even stop fully at every stop sign! I have achieved great success and maintained integrity!"

You and I would be ready to hit such a person! What pride in his heritage and accomplishments! Yet, those are the sentiments of Paul—before he found Christ. Before Christ—"B.C."—Paul took great pride in his pedigree and achievements. He was the Jewish epitome of success, religiously speaking.

Paul's zealousness reminds me of an article in the *Los Angeles Times* that told about the Jewish women of Jerusalem and their cleaning efforts before Passover. Talk about accomplishments! Author Marjorie Miller writes about "spring cleaning run amok": a month-long ritual housecleaning because of Jewish law that requires a house to be purged of all traces of *hametz*, or leavening, before Passover begins. Miller explains, "Women turn their houses upside down, beating rugs, emptying closets and whitewashing walls. They pull clean dishes from cupboards to boil them, scrape the cracks between floor tiles and even dust spines of books, in case a family member has eaten a cookie while studying sometime during the year."[2]

The men (and, of course, few men are involved in the cleaning) are the "cheerleaders" for all this activity. Former Chief Rabbi

Mordechai Eliyahu lectured women in the Mahane Yehuda neighbor-hood recently and said, "If there is a crumb in the kitchen hiding in the corner, you should do everything to remove it. If need be, you should take a hammer and chisel and destroy the wall until the crumb comes out."[3]

The article does mention those who regard the law with more balance, but I was fascinated by this spring cleaning ritual. If I were a part of that culture, I would be leading the charge to get rid of anything that might break the law. Then I could add it to my list of accomplishments.

But, thank God, I don't have to keep the letter of the Law to consider myself significant in God's eyes. I am significant and important regardless of whether or not I keep my house clean.

In the same way, Paul had tried to keep his human "house" free from spiritual "leaven." After meeting Christ personally, however, he became willing to exchange his earthly values of respect from others, the privileges of righteous standing, the comfort of wealth, the self-satisfaction of pride, and the efforts of self. He traded them for true satisfaction, peace, contentment, and lasting joy.

Dr. Herbert Lockyer said, "God has set eternity in the heart of man (Ecclesiastes 3:11, RSV), and thus no earthly splendor or wealth can ever fully satisfy that heart."[4] If we buy into an earthly perspective that "achievements define who I am," then we will ulti-mately be disappointed. The satisfaction from such achievements is fleeting and dependent upon succeeding and gaining more and more. But a heavenly perspective brings satisfaction because it is based on something much more solid: an identity as a child of God, something that never changes or becomes devalued.

A Princess of the King

I remember the summer I felt constantly tired. I couldn't figure out why I didn't have any energy. Because I had a deadline for a book, I forced myself to continue writing every day. Eventually, however,

I became so drained that I made an appointment with my doctor. Through a blood test, I discovered that I had mononucleosis.

When I inquired how long it might last, my doctor said it was different for each person. I hoped my body could fight it quickly. That book still needed to be finished and I had many wonderful speaking engagements scheduled for the fall. I just couldn't imagine not making my deadline or fulfilling my speaking commitments. And the thought of being inactive was very threatening. I thought, "I love it all too much. It's who I am. How will I feel about myself if I can't accomplish things?"

Plus, I couldn't imagine the Lord not wanting me to keep the speaking engagements He'd given me. Being dependable was very important to me. If I canceled an event, wouldn't that mean I was undependable? Could I allow people to think that way about me? All these thoughts and confused feelings swirled in my mind as I contemplated the repercussions of my illness.

In the midst of my speculations, I realized I had little choice. I had no energy! I could hardly move without feeling completely exhausted. Correspondence was piling up on my desk. My manuscript languished. My family wanted attention I couldn't give. Empty feelings of uselessness pecked away at my self-image. *I can't do anything. I can't accomplish anything. What good am I?*

As one week and then several weeks passed and I didn't feel any better, I began to understand that this was going to be a long struggle. *Lord,* I prayed, *You know how much I enjoy getting things done. I hate to say it, but I base a lot of my self-image and identity on all that. Can I handle this?*

I knew that if this had happened years earlier, I would have drowned in feelings of uselessness. But over many years, God had been teaching me that my identity was not based in "doing," but in "being" a child of His. Now would I pass the test? How would I deal with this season of inactivity?

As I spent most of my time sleeping or reading, the earthly idea would niggle that I was insignificant without accomplishments. But deep down I still felt valued by God even though I did little. I recognized that all my work and ministry was not the most important thing about me. God didn't need me to be doing those things. What He "needed" was my fellowship with Him. He wanted me to know that my true identity was "in Christ," not in activity.

My weeks in bed—and then a gradual strengthening over a course of nine months—taught me a lot. I learned again, as I must over and over, that I could count all my work, ministry, and accomplishments "a loss compared to the surpassing greatness of knowing Christ Jesus my Lord," just as the apostle Paul did.

Paul's use of the word "count" has the sense of "evaluate or assess." Paul evaluated everything he had before Christ and everything he gained through knowing Christ, and he could say without a doubt that the present knowledge of Christ was far superior. In fact, he considers everything from "B.C." rubbish! That strong word is the same as "excrement, food thrown away which is useless and actually contaminating and harmful."

I think it's significant that his words in Philippians were penned thirty years after his Damascus road experience. We're not talking about new convert excitement here. Paul remembers what his earthly perspective involved, and yet through thirty years of "evaluating," he confirmed that Christ offers the best!

I look back on my season of "being still and knowing God" and consider it a precious experience of deepening my intimacy with Him through silence and inactivity. I am encouraged to know that the important thing in life is to focus not on my accomplishments, but on my inheritance in Christ as a princess of the King.

Of course, I don't always remember this! I often still regard certain things as the source of my value and significance. For example, being considered athletic has always been important to me. When I recently played softball on our adult fellowship team, I initially pictured myself getting at least a base hit. When I couldn't even hit past the infield and botched catching a fly ball in the outfield, I felt my enthusiasm for the church picnic deflating like a balloon with a slow leak. I didn't like the fact that facing fifty had diminished my image as an athlete.

Over and over God has to remind me that I must learn to place more importance on whose I am than in what I do. My aptitudes and accomplishments change, but my inheritance in Christ will never be diminished. Nothing—absolutely nothing—is more significant than the fact that I am a child of God.

Author Chuck Swindoll challenges us in this way:

> For me to live is money and to die is to leave it all behind.
>
> For me to live is fame and to die is to be quickly forgotten.
>
> For me to live is power and influence and to die is to lose both.
>
> For me to live is possessions and to die is to depart with nothing in my hands.
>
> Somehow, they all fall flat, don't they? When money is our objective, we must live in fear of losing it, which makes us paranoid and suspicious. When fame is our aim, we become competitive lest others upstage us, which makes us envious. When power and influence drive us, we become self-serving and strong-willed, which makes us arrogant. And when possessions become our God, we become materialistic, thinking enough is never enough, which makes us greedy. All these pursuits fly in the face of contentment . . . and joy.
>
> Only Christ can satisfy, whether we have or don't have, whether we are known or unknown, whether we live or die. And the good news is this: Death only sweetens the pie![5]

What ultimately must define us is our inheritance in Christ because it never changes, disappoints, or dissolves. It is immutable, secure, powerful, steadfast, and always available.

A Glorious Inheritance

Along with Paul, I think of two examples from the Bible that contrast those who value their inheritance in Christ and those who don't. Esau is a man who didn't value his spiritual birthright. Lydia was someone who could clearly see that being "in Christ" could give someone his or her identity. Let's look first at Esau, whose story is told in Genesis 25:29-34.

It may have been a dusty kind of day when Esau arrived home famished and exhausted. The sweat from his trip caked his skin, his stomach growled ferociously, and he couldn't wait to eat. Everything sounded good, even his own cooking!

As he entered the tent, a fabulous aroma greeted his nostrils. Jacob was making that delicious stew of his again. What perfect timing! Esau's stomach turned flip-flops in anticipation of the great meal he would have.

"Jacob!" he called. "I'm absolutely starved. Give me some of your wonderful stew. I'm so weak, I can hardly take another step until I have something to eat."

Jacob began ladling the stew into a bowl, then paused. An idea bounced into his mind and he knew it was a winner. "Okay, Esau," he replied, "but first you have to sell me your rights as the firstborn."

Esau stopped in his tracks—not because he was exhausted, which he was, but because he was stunned by Jacob's demand. *My birthright? What brought that on?* he wondered. He paused for a moment and the exhaustion seeped deeper into his bones. "I've got to eat or else I'll die," he muttered. "What good is my inheritance if I'm dead?

"All right, Jacob," Esau said as he collapsed onto a rug. "You can have my birthright. Now give me that food, I tell you!"

"No," Jacob countered, "you have to swear to it!"

"Whatever! I swear that by you giving me this food, I've sold you my inheritance as the firstborn. It's yours, Okay? Just give me the stew. I'm gonna die!"

Seconds later, as Esau scooped the delicious stew into his

mouth, he thought it was the best food he'd ever tasted. It wasn't until some time later that the loss of his birthright brought a bad taste into his mouth when he didn't receive the blessing he desired from his father. His temporary hunger had become more important to him than a spiritual birthright that would bless his life forever. He would regret his snap decision the rest of his days.

In contrast, Lydia is a woman described in Acts 16:13-15 who was willing to acknowledge her need of a spiritual inheritance. Perhaps her salvation happened like this.

Lydia arrived at the riverside and greeted the other women. They were a varied lot from different backgrounds, but their desire to seek God was their common bond. Because Philippi didn't have the required ten men to establish a synagogue, the women met on the Sabbath day for prayer by the river, a common location for worship. As each of the women seated herself on her favorite rock, Lydia thoughtfully reflected on her journey toward God. She was a Gentile who recognized Jehovah as the true God. Yet there was still something unsettled in her soul.

Lydia was the most successful of the women there and yet her success did not satisfy her. She once thought it would. She could remember telling her sister many years ago, "Just wait until my business really takes off, then I'll be successful and happy. I'm going to be just like Sonia. Remember her?"

Her sister had nodded, remembering their mother's successful friend who was a seller of purple cloth. She had a head for business and a strong personality. She was respected and clever, never letting anyone trick her out of anything.

"But Lydia, Sonia never seemed happy to me. Do you really want to be like her?"

"I'm going to have the rich part and also be happy. Just you wait."

Yet now Lydia had more money than Sonia ever had and she still wasn't happy. It bothered her that her little sister had been so insightful. She just didn't think it would turn out like this. But she could see God's hand. Her dissatisfaction with her success had driven her to seek Jehovah. But she still felt she was lacking something. That bothered her.

As the women began their silent prayers, they were suddenly interrupted by three men who approached their small group. At first Lydia's heart leapt with joy. Men! Maybe they could establish a synagogue soon. But then she realized there weren't enough of them. *Oh, well, at least it's a start,* she thought. The men introduced themselves as Paul, Luke, and Silas. Paul, who seemed to be the leader, addressed the women, asking them questions about the area and the beliefs of the local Jews.

After some conversation, Paul began to explain that they represented a new division of the Jews called "The Way." At first when this funny-looking man began talking about someone named Jesus and identified Him as the Messiah, Lydia felt suspicious. If the Messiah had actually come, why hadn't they heard about it? Her business sense warned her that these men might be looking for money. She knew she should be cautious, but as they spoke of this "Son of God" who had performed miracles, and how He died and then was raised again from the dead, she felt her heart pounding with anticipation.

"Now, don't get carried away, Lydia," her sensible mind warned. But the more she heard, the more she saw the significance of it. She hungered for more and could tell that the other women did too. For once she was hearing of a proposition that was too good to be true—but it was!

Before she knew it, she confessed, "You have persuaded me. I do believe this man Jesus is the Son of God and died for my sins on that cross. What must I do to be saved?"

Within minutes, several of the women, including herself, had gone with the apostle into the river and were baptized. Lydia's heart was overflowing with joy and gratitude. No longer did she feel that dissatisfaction and emptiness. She didn't care whether she was rich or poor. She belonged to God, and Paul explained that she was now a "new creature in Christ." Well, whatever that meant, she knew she wanted to know more.

"Come to my house and stay," she urged the men.

"But there are three of us. Do you have room?"

She laughed. "Oh, yes, my house is very large. The servants will be glad to get your rooms ready. It's the least I can do for the spiritual life and peace you have showed me. I know for sure that all I've accomplished is nothing compared to the joy of knowing God through His Son Jesus. And besides, I want my children and servants to hear about this Jesus also." So the group gathered their belongings and walked to Lydia's house.

For Paul, Lydia, and all of us who know the goodness of God through salvation, nothing compares to the joy of knowing Jesus if that's what we're really focused on. Unlike Esau, we realize that personal success and accomplishments give a temporary peace and joy, but it doesn't last. Only a growing relationship with God through identifying with Christ brings permanent satisfaction.

The more we focus on our identity in Christ, the more we appreciate what God has done for us. Whether we are rich or poor, successful or just getting by, full of energy or slowed by illness, the solid foundation in our lives is knowing that our inheritance as a Christian will never diminish in value and actually is "who I am."

Our spiritual birthright secures for us countless treasures, including these gems:

- I have peace in the midst of a troubled world (John 14:27).
- I am justified through faith (Romans 5:1).
- I am an ambassador for Christ (2 Corinthians 5:20).
- I have every spiritual blessing in Christ (Ephesians 1:3).
- I am holy and blameless in God's sight (Ephesians 1:4).
- I am adopted as His child (Ephesians 1:5).
- I am forgiven of all my sins— past, present, and future (Ephesians 1:7).
- God has prepared in advance the good things He wants me to do for His glory (Ephesians 2:10).

Each aspect of our inheritance helps us to see ourselves the way God sees us: as His chosen princesses, daughters of the King. As heirs in His heavenly kingdom, we are entitled to everything we need for living as royalty.

My writer friend Donna Goodrich communicates this truth so effectively through this little reflection:

> The bedspread was ugly. I had bought it in desperation at a garage sale for $5.00. "Yuk," I said, each time I made the bed. I grimaced as I spread the cover.
>
> Then one day I was leafing through my sister's JC Penney catalog. There was the same bedspread with a well-known designer name. $85.00! Suddenly the bedspread took on a new beauty—once I discovered how much it cost.
>
> At one time I didn't think much of myself. I felt ugly. "Yuk," I said each time I looked in the mirror.
>
> Then one day I heard the story of salvation—how Christ had given His life on Calvary, just for me. And suddenly my life took on a new beauty—once I discovered how much it cost.[6]

Donna has given us a word picture of our value in Christ, which is the basis of our inheritance in Him. Let's explore a couple of the treasures included in this glorious inheritance that I think are particularly liberating.

Complete Acceptance

For me, Colossians 2.10 is one of the most meaningful elements of my inheritance in Christ: "In Him you have been made complete." That word "complete" carries with it the idea of being perfect. In God's eyes, you and I are perfect. There's nothing we can do to make ourselves more acceptable to God. It's already been done to the max! And because we had nothing to do with it—other than asking Jesus Christ to come into our lives as Lord and Savior—it can't be taken away.

This ingredient of our inheritance replaces the feeling that we are unacceptable to God unless we accomplish things. It is particularly important to me because of my childhood beliefs that I had to be good enough and do well enough to be acceptable to God. Even as a Christian, I've struggled with thoughts like:

"I haven't had my devotions today; I didn't spend enough time with God. He can't be pleased with me."

"I don't love that person enough. God wants me to love completely. He's most likely stopped loving me because of it."

"My heart isn't wholly devoted to God. See how I make wrong choices? There's no hope for me."

These condemning accusations have robbed me of peace. Yet God has continually reminded me, "My daughter, you are already complete in My eyes. Relax and let Me work in you. Yes, I'll need your cooperation, but stop thinking you must perform perfectly for Me to love you without reservation. Even if you could complete all sorts of spiritual feats, I still couldn't love you more than I do right now."

That kind of total acceptance has helped me to feel more secure and loved. Little by little, my need to accomplish has been replaced with a deep sense of God's unconditional acceptance.

If you are still feeling like you need to perform to earn or deserve God's love, read chapter 2 again and claim your inheritance in Christ by embracing this truth: "I am complete and perfect, not because I achieve certain goals, but because Jesus' robe of righteousness is wrapped around me."

Perfect Guidance

Do you sometimes feel confused? Unable to discern right from wrong? Swayed by the ideas of the people around you? Do you wonder how to respond to people or circumstances when life throws a curve? If you're depending upon your accomplishments or your previous experience to give you the answers, you may or may not know what to do.

But take heart. The answer can be found in an aspect of your inheritance in Christ as explained in 2 Timothy 3:16-17: "All Scripture is inspired by God and profitable for teaching, for reproof, for correction, for training in righteousness; that the man of God may be adequate, equipped for every good work." God has provided His children with the means to know and do His will. In His Word we will always find guidance for every situation.

Some time ago, I experienced one of those challenges of not knowing how to respond. Initially, I wanted to react out of my own earthly thinking, but having seen the futility of that in the past, I decided I wanted to behave in a godly fashion. But how could I do that? Let me tell you what happened.

A women's ministry team of a nearby church had invited me to speak at their retreat. I was particularly thrilled with this invitation because I had wanted to speak at that church for a long time. Somehow in my mind, I had built up such an opportunity as a real accomplishment—something that would indicate I was a good speaker.

After the invitation came, I met with the ministry team, trying to determine their needs. They approved my suggestions and also invited me to speak at another event, three months prior to the retreat. I spoke at the preliminary event and was thrilled with the response of the women. But two months before the retreat, one of the team members called to say they were canceling me as the retreat speaker. I couldn't believe it. Why? She explained that they were looking for a Bible teacher and I wasn't that style.

I tried desperately to salvage the opportunity by saying I could also do that. In my mind I was screaming, "But you didn't tell me that's what you wanted!" She was unconvinced, and after the conversation concluded, I sat crying in a pile of despair. Why didn't they tell me? I thought I followed God's leading. It was so difficult dealing with the different team members at different times. Did they pass along my comments and questions so that everyone was aware of everything I'd said? Why didn't they realize that I could rise to whatever challenge they put before me? I agonized over our conversation. I felt like a failure. I also felt humiliated. The church was in my local area. Everyone was going to find out they canceled me. *There goes my reputation!* I despaired. *No one will ever ask me to speak again.* As I looked at the situation through my earthly lenses, I thought my ministry was dead in the water.

As I struggled to prevent depression from clouding my trust in God, I told myself, "Kathy, you've been canceled before; it's no big deal." But somehow this *was* a big deal. This group was large and the church was highly respected. In my mind, it was one of those special opportunities. *I guess I'm just not special enough to have it,* I thought.

As I fought to regain an eternal perspective, I recalled basic principles from the Bible regarding how I should respond. I shouldn't be so angry. I should trust God. I should learn from this experience and not put my value into a certain speaking opportunity. It all sounded right, but my spirit and pride were wounded. I felt confused and unable to concentrate.

But then I remembered the experience of a friend who, during a recent time of being wounded, told me how she'd turned immediately to the Bible for specific help. She had also been rejected in a Christian setting and told me she'd had a godly response only because of the time she spent with God searching the Scriptures for the guidance she needed.

While I could mentally recall biblical principles, my friend's example reminded me that a quick review from memory wasn't as powerful as actually reading and searching God's Word for help in a specific situation. So in the midst of my tears and grief, I opened my Bible and turned to Philippians 2. It came alive with specific instruction. I read, "Do nothing from selfishness or empty conceit, but with humility of mind let each of you regard one another as more important than himself" (verse 3). And "Have this attitude in yourselves which was also in Christ Jesus" (verse 5). And "He humbled Himself by becoming obedient to the point of death, even death on a cross" (verse 8). Of course, I "knew" the principles stated there, but suddenly, in a way that I can't describe, the words penetrated my hurting heart and comforted me, strengthening me to choose humility and a Christ-like response. I couldn't have had that response on my own without taking advantage of this treasure included in my spiritual birthright—the perfect instruction and guidance of God's Word.

As I meditated on those verses in Philippians 2, God revealed that I had replaced my value in Christ with the accomplishment of speaking at that particular church. No wonder the disappointment had hit me with such force. A false sense of my self-esteem, my value, and my significance were being threatened. In reviewing the truth that a speaking engagement did not determine my value, I could again focus on my inheritance in Christ as a princess of the King. God affirmed that He still loved me and meant this experience for my good.

As I basked in His love, I also sensed Him saying, "Don't defend yourself." That was the hardest thing for me to hear! I wanted with everything inside me to call and convince those women they were making a mistake. But reading how Jesus had emptied Himself of His own reputation gave me the strength to submit to God's will and stay quiet. Even as I received a few consoling calls from friends who had heard, I resisted being bitter. I can't say all the pain was gone immediately, but in time it gradually diminished. The truth of Hebrews 4:12 proved itself: "For the word of God is living and active and sharper than any two-edged sword, and piercing as far as the division of soul and spirit, of both joints and marrow, and able to judge the thoughts and intentions of the heart."

Are you wondering how you should respond to criticism? Or maybe you know someone is spreading a lie about you. What should you do? Are you trying to decide whether to accept a particular responsibility or to make a significant purchase? The next time you face confusion, discouragement, or uncertainty, open the Word of God. Seek your answers there. His truth will pierce your heart and empower you from the inside out to respond in a godly manner to life's challenges and choices.

Reveling in Our Spiritual Identity

Knowing about our inheritance as children of God and living out the implications are two different things, aren't they? When I think of the importance of actually applying what I know, I remember an experience I had while on vacation. I'd left our hotel room for some exercise and became annoyed when a large seed pod got caught in the sole of my running shoe. Every time I put my foot down while running, the seed pod not only made a crunching noise, it was awkward—like stepping on a rock. I repeatedly tried to dislodge the annoyance from my shoe but it stuck fast. Finally, I broke one of my fingernails trying to get it free. I was irritated and wondered, "How can I get this thing to stop bothering me?"

My hand brushed against the side of my shorts and I felt something hard in my pocket. "Oh, I have my hotel room key!" I remembered as I pulled it out of my pocket. "I can use it to dislodge the seed!" I quickly and easily applied the tip of the key to the edge of the seed pod and it popped out of the sole. Amazing!

In that moment, as I again took off running, I realized that was a visual picture of the importance of my inheritance in Christ. I had been ineffective in dislodging that seed pod and didn't take advantage of the resource that lay unnoticed in my pocket. When I did use the key, I was freed from my annoying running partner. Likewise, when you and I don't effectively draw on our inherited spiritual blessings, we are impotent in dealing with the annoyances, temptations, and difficulties of life. When we forget about our spiritual resources, we naturally fall back on our own efforts—which are never adequate.

Replacing our earthly perspective with a heavenly one doesn't happen overnight. My perspective on my personal identity in Christ has changed over many years, primarily as a result of spending extended time with God and of correcting wrong beliefs about His nature. I don't think we can experience life-altering changes in our thinking unless we study God's attributes as they are described in the Bible and become intimate with God in quiet time each day. For me, a daily focused time with God and a monthly extended time are the keys to spiritual growth. Reading and studying the Bible, along with praying each day, keeps me on the path to knowing Him in spirit and in truth. It's during those times that He points out through His Word or by the whisper of His Spirit that I am not looking at life from His perspective. I'm depending on my own accomplishments instead of on His abundant provision. Then I know it's time to reorient my thinking and remember the wonderful privileges I can enjoy as God's child.

Over the years I have experienced a subtle but significant change from valuing myself based on my accomplishments and my "image" to valuing myself because I'm a precious princess of the King. One experience in particular is evidence of how far God has brought me in this area.

It all started when, as a child, I came to some conclusions about God that were not correct. I was in third grade and I was very proud of my new permanent front teeth. They were straight and pretty and I felt good about myself because of them. But one day, when running on the asphalt playground at school, I tripped and fell flat on my face, shattering those two perfect teeth. Because my jaw hadn't finished forming, the dentist covered over the sharp points that were left with silver temporary caps. I felt ashamed of my appearance and suffered the mocking of my peers any time I smiled.

God made this happen, I reasoned. *He doesn't love me, and He certainly can't be trusted.* In my emotional pain, I began to form an earthly perspective about God's nature: He was mean and capricious. More "evidence" to support this negative view of God came through additional dental disappointments as I grew up. Three teeth were pulled because of an abscess, and for many years I wore a removable partial plate.

During those years I tried desperately to be good enough to earn God's love, while still holding onto my belief that He really wasn't someone I could count on. Eventually I was fitted for a permanent bridge, and when I accepted Christ as my Savior at the age of eighteen, my wrong ideas about God began to change. My adult life has been a journey deeper into the heart of His grace. But seven years ago, God handed me another "tooth test" that would prove my reliance on Him alone!

One morning I noticed that one side of my bridge was loose. My dentist explained after examining me, "Since the tooth has broken, we'll have to drill down two more teeth, one on each side, to attach a new bridge." He paused, looking thoughtful. "But you do have another option. You could consider dental implants."

My periodontist, Dr. Gaffaney, explained more about the procedure. The initial surgery would install the titanium implants into my jaw. Then during the four to six months it took for my bone to grow around the implants and secure them, I would wear a temporary partial plate. Later the permanent teeth would be attached to the implants.

I opted for the implants and set the surgery date. I explained to Dr. Gaffaney that I was a professional speaker and that my next speaking engagement was just ten days after my initial surgery was scheduled. He assured me that would be no problem since by then my gums would be healed enough for me to wear the partial plate. And indeed, it wouldn't have been a problem except that during surgery, Dr. Gaffaney discovered that one side of my jaw was too thin and he had to put in a bone graft. That made wearing the partial plate dangerous because it could bump against the graft and dislodge it.

During one of my visits shortly after surgery, Dr. Gaffaney told me I should let the meeting planner for my speaking engagement know I might not be able to speak—in case I still couldn't wear the partial plate. I did, and the meeting planner said she would be praying I'd be able to come.

The meeting was scheduled for Monday evening, and that previous Friday I was preparing my material in case I could speak. Suddenly I sensed the Lord whisper in my heart, "You're going to go without your teeth."

I shook my head in disbelief. I certainly couldn't have heard correctly. "Oh, Father, I don't think they want to have a speaker without her three top front teeth."

But almost simultaneously, I felt a peace envelop my body and spirit. I looked down at the plans for my talk and realized that my missing front teeth could be the visual aid for the point of my message. An excitement and anticipation of God's working made me hope I *would* have to go without my teeth! For sure, the women would never forget the speaker without her front teeth.

Well, you guessed it: Not only did I go to that speaking engagement without my teeth, but to many others over the following month as my mouth healed. At one of those events, the retreat committee introduced me by singing, "All I want for Christmas are my three front teeth."

During that month, I was awed to recognize the changes in my thinking about the nature of God. As a child, I'd concluded that God was unloving and untrustworthy because of my teeth-shattering accident. Now I was speaking before hundreds of people without my front teeth and believed without a doubt that God loved me and that He could be trusted. I had become convinced of the truth of 1 John 4:18: "There is no fear in love; but perfect love casts out fear." I could trust God's love because it was perfect: He wanted only the best for me, with or without teeth! I had exchanged my earthly perspective for an eternal one.

The same transformation can take place in your mind and heart if you are willing to count your personal accomplishments as "rubbish" compared to the incomparable value of knowing Christ and the treasures of His kingdom. Then when someone asks you, "Who are you?" you can answer, "I'm a daughter of the King of heaven, a princess in His eternal kingdom." At least you'll get her attention!

✣ *Questions* ✣

1. Have you thought in the past that certain efforts or accomplishments could gain you an identity as someone of value and importance? What changed that perspective or what needs to change about that perspective?

2. Read Paul's description of his life before Christ in Philippians 3:4-6. In what ways have you tried to become righteous on your own?

3. What things, activities, or accomplishments does God want you to count as loss for the sake of Christ?

4. Although Greta Garbo's comment on page 34 may seem extreme, we each can have something apart from Christ that is important enough to us to make huge sacrifices for. Is there anything like that in your life?

5. How important to you is the value of knowing Christ? In what practical way do you demonstrate that? Some examples are Bible study, prayer, discovering and eliminating wrong ideas about the nature of God, and concentrating on His qualities and attributes. In what specific ways would you like to give Him a place of greater importance in your life?

6. Which inheritance in Christ listed on pages 44-45 do you value the most? Why?

7. Which inheritance is most difficult for you to believe or accept? Why?

8. What can you do to begin to believe or accept it more?

9. If someone were to ask you, "Who are you?" how would you answer? What does your response say about your relationship with God?

4

Faith

*God is in loving control of my life
and wants only the best for me.*

God has no problems, only plans.

CORRIE TEN BOOM

I do not believe that sheer suffering teaches. If suffering
alone taught, all the world would be wise, since
everyone suffers. To suffering must be added mourning,
understanding, patience, love, openness, and the
willingness to remain vulnerable.

ANNE MORROW LINDBERGH

*J*IM AND BONNIE JEFFERS EXPECTED THAT THEIR HOME WOULD sell quickly. Jim had been hired as assistant pastor at a church in Lake Arrowhead, California. Their home in Whittier, ninety miles away, had been priced by their real estate agent well below market to ensure a quick sale. The agent held open houses, advertised heavily, and did everything possible to sell the house. Week after week Bonnie and Jim received no offers, no interest, and no potential buyers.

Meanwhile they were house-sitting at various places in Lake Arrowhead with no home to call their own—not an optimum way to begin a ministry in a new area. They kept asking the Lord, "Why don't you act? It just doesn't make sense to us. We've obeyed you by taking on this ministry but the stress is making it too difficult. Please bring a buyer for our home!"

After months of fruitless pleading with the Lord, they finally gave up, rented out their Whittier house, and found a place to rent near their new church. For almost two years, a seminary couple enjoyed renting the Jeffers' close-to-the-school, reasonably-priced home.

About the time the renters headed for the mission field, Jim entered a doctoral program near their original home and resigned from the Lake Arrowhead church. Jim and Bonnie moved back into their Whittier home while Jim finished school. Not long after that they listed their house—for twice the price of two years earlier. It sold in less than three weeks in a bidding war between two potential buyers.

Bonnie looks back on that time of wondering whether God was really in control of their lives and now knows He certainly was and continues to be! In time, their initial earthly perspective of fretting over God's ability to sell their home became a heavenly perspective of seeing that a good and loving God had a better plan. He knew exactly what He wanted to do; the Jeffers just had to walk through it. As a result, their faith and dependence upon God deepened.

None of us escapes the kind of questions the Jeffers had: Is God really in control when my problems aren't easily solved? Does God care about me and my struggles when the strength I need is slow in coming? Is God good when trial after trial assails me and there's no relief for my pain?

While we're in the midst of problems, it's easy to allow an earthly perspective of doubting God's goodness to blur our trust and faith in Him. But if we'll practice refocusing on the truth that God is in loving control and wants only the best for us, we will keep our heavenly glasses perched on our spiritual noses.

When Jesus Is Late

We're most tempted to remove those glasses of trusting God when He delays in answering our prayers. When we're in pain, we want relief—now! We cry out, "Where is Your help, God? If You really love me and want the best for me, why don't You intervene?" Author Charles Stanley writes, "I don't know that I have met anyone who likes to wait. We live in the 'now generation.' We expect and want solutions immediately. We dislike the tension and uncertainty that waiting typically involves."[1]

That may have been the way Mary and Martha felt as they faced Lazarus' death in John 11. Their response represents the way most of us view life with an earthly perspective. When Lazarus fell sick, Mary and Martha demonstrated their faith by quickly calling for Jesus. That's to their credit. They believed with all their might that Jesus could and would heal Lazarus. They couldn't imagine that their friendship with the Son of God wouldn't spare them from the pain of having their beloved brother die.

But Jesus didn't come. We can only speculate about the sisters' perplexity, but can't you just picture Martha, the more active woman, walking out the front door a hundred times a day, peering down the dusty road, expecting to see Jesus trudging, even hurrying along, to relieve them of their pain? "Why isn't He here yet?" she cries out to Mary, throwing up her hands in disbelief.

"Oh, Martha, I'm sure He'll be here soon. He won't forsake us. He loves Lazarus too much."

"Then why isn't He here?" Martha demands, wringing her hands. She runs to the window again, squinting her eyes. "Oh, I think I see Him," she exclaims. "Yes, it's Him!"

Martha and Mary run out of the house and down the walkway but realize it's not Jesus walking up the road. It's their neighbor, coming to check on Lazarus. Their shoulders slumped, they shuffle back into the house.

Mary rests her hand on Martha's shoulder and says, "There must be a good reason He hasn't come, Martha. You know He wouldn't forget us."

Martha's furrowed brow shadows angry eyes. "What could be more important than His friend Lazarus?" she asks. She couldn't add "and us" without appearing selfish—but she wanted to.

Finally, in her pain, she spits out, "I thought He loved us. I guess I was wrong." As Martha stomps into the house, Mary stands shaking her head, muttering, "Martha, Martha. . . . "

And then it happens. Lazarus dies. Up to the very last moment, the sisters continued to search the horizon for their Savior's familiar form, knowing that no matter how late He came, He could and would restore Lazarus' health. But now Lazarus is dead. Even Jesus can't do anything about that. It's final. Over. Grief and hurt mingle in the women's eyes. If only Jesus had come.

And then He arrives. Late. Four days after Lazarus was buried.

We know the rest of the story and its glorious results, but in that moment, Martha and Mary didn't. They believed in the future resurrection for Lazarus and themselves, but to expect Jesus to bring him back from the dead was beyond their imagination. Yet that's exactly what He does, and God is given greater glory than if He had arrived on time to wipe away the pain of illness and prevent death.

I take great comfort in the way Jesus responds to Martha's plaintive rebuke, "Lord, if You had been here, my brother would not have died" (John 11:21). Jesus, knowing the sisters' pain and perplexity at His delay, doesn't reprimand them or tell them to not feel the way they do. He had a purpose in His delay and now He'll let them in on the fabulous plan.

Mary and Martha were Jesus' good friends and they believed in His power and love. They thought that should add up to receiving His attention and healing hand upon their beloved brother. It's easy for us to criticize their shortsightedness since we can read the end of the story within a few verses, but many times we show the same earthly perspective when God doesn't answer our prayers in a timely fashion. Like Mary and Martha, we may feel abandoned during those times when God's answer comes slowly or seemingly late. But Isaiah 55:8-9 reminds us that God's outlook is far beyond our ability to comprehend: "'For My thoughts are not your thoughts, Neither are your ways My ways,' declares the LORD. 'For as the heavens are higher than the earth, So are My ways higher than your ways, And My thoughts than your thoughts.'" Mary and Martha didn't see God's higher point of view until after Lazarus was raised. They thought they would have been content to have him healed, but Jesus had a much more dramatic and glorious plan.

Charles Stanley writes, "Always, in God's omniscient mind, He uses seasons of waiting to prepare us for His answer. We want the object of our desire now, but God knows we must sift through our motives, check the counsel of other godly men and women, or simply wait until He has orchestrated all the necessary components to bless us and others involved in our decision."[2]

How is God using your waiting time? Are you maturing? Are you becoming stronger in your faith? Are you seeking Him above instant gratification? As Mary and Martha discovered, you can trust that He loves you and knows exactly what He's doing to bring the ultimate good into your life.

God Even Uses Sin

When you and I are in pain, as Mary and Martha were, we usually can't conceive of how God can use our circumstances for good. That is especially true when our pain is the result of our own sin. We can quote Romans 8:28 to ourselves, yet there seems to be a set of parentheses in that verse: "And we know that God causes all things (except what I'm going through) to work together for good to those who love God, to those who are called according to His purpose."

That was my attitude more than twenty years ago, as I struggled in the grip of abusive anger. Even though I'd been a Christian for ten years at the time, I couldn't lay hold of God's power. I was intensely dissatisfied and frustrated that my husband didn't fulfill all my expectations. We had been married seven years and Larry still had interests beyond just making me happy! He worked two jobs, as a policeman and real estate agent, plus he had a flying hobby. He was rarely home and I was furious at his insensitivity. Because he had led me to the Lord when we were dating and God had brought him into my life to be my "Prince Charming," I thought our marriage would—and should—be perfect and satisfying.

Instead, I was stuck at home with a very active, strong-willed two-year-old daughter, Darcy, and infant son, Mark. The angrier I became at Larry, the more I took it out on Darcy—to the point that I physically abused her. I knew I was wrong and I hated myself.

Over and over again I prayed for deliverance from my anger. "Surely, God, this isn't too hard for You. Why won't You take away my anger? I don't want to be this kind of mother! I want to be a perfect mother!" When God didn't answer my prayer instantaneously, I concluded He didn't care and didn't love me anymore. I fell deeper into my pit of anger and despair.

But over several years, God proved His faithfulness. Whereas I had wanted immediate deliverance, God's different plan was to take me through a process of growth. I thought He didn't love me because He hadn't answered my prayer in my way. I was about to learn that He always answers prayers—in His way.

In the first year, He strengthened me to control my physical abuse. Within another year, I'd stopped my verbal abuse. Little by little, He revealed to me the underlying causes of my anger. He also gave me the courage to share my struggle at the ladies neighborhood Bible study that I led. I learned to forgive myself and believe that God wanted to forgive me. I identified myself as a perfectionist and discovered how to discipline a toddler without anger. The more I learned, the more I depended upon God for the next step. I was definitely "in process." Eventually, God delivered me from my anger and pain.

And then He opened doors I could have never imagined. He gave me opportunities to minister to other hurting parents through writing and speaking. What I had learned during my process of healing, I could now share with others. God certainly hadn't desired Darcy's hurt at my hands, but He redeemed the experience in my life and in Darcy's. His plan for Darcy is still unfolding. She doesn't remember the abuse she suffered, but she encourages me to speak and write about it so that other families can be helped. She even shares the books I've written about the abuse and healing with her friends. She's at peace and has never tried to use my past behavior against me. Recently, we even wrote a book together called *Staying Friends With Your Kids*. Darcy is a willing vessel and I have no doubt that God will continue to use her life in ways that glorify Him.

God has also used that pain for good for Larry and me. We just recently celebrated our twenty-ninth anniversary and adore each other. As best friends and as coauthors and speakers, we love ministering and being together. As we share in our book, *When the Honeymoon's Over*, in the early years of our marriage we were each looking to the other to meet our needs completely. I, especially, was operating under the banner, "I got Larry to the altar, now I'll alter him." My strategy was to change him to be who I needed him to be. But when I surrendered that philosophy (but that's another story) and realized that only God could meet my needs, I became a more positive person to live with. Gone was the nagging, discontent, and clinging to Larry as my source of happiness. As I released Larry and responded to him differently, he noticed and wanted to spend more time with me. Then we attended a couples' retreat and began the process God used to restore our relationship. We still had a lot to learn, but God guided us through it. We discovered that with Christ there is always hope, even for a troubled relationship.

While still in my pit of anger and despair, I believed the lie that God didn't care about me or my pain. Yet, like Mary and Martha, I eventually saw a far greater glory in Jesus appearing "late." I am now convinced that there are no parentheses in Romans 8:28. *Everything* can be used by God when we turn our pain over to Him. Even our own sin is a vehicle for Him to display His glory and bring good into our lives. Regardless of what we're facing, God is endlessly creative in His ability to use our pain for His glory and our growth.

Rejoicing in Trials

As we practice looking at life through our heavenly glasses, the apostle Paul's words about suffering begin to make sense: "Not only so, but we also rejoice in our sufferings, because we know that suffering produces perseverance; perseverance, character; and character, hope. And hope does not disappoint us, because God has poured out his love into our hearts by the Holy Spirit, whom he has given us" (Romans 5:3-5).

When we're struggling, we can see only glimmers of the beautiful character and precious hope God is painting onto the canvas of our souls. Some time ago, I received from a friend a little canvas on which she had painted a scene of a boat sailing along the coast. When I held the small picture close to me, it didn't look very beautiful because the different colors didn't seem to blend. But when

I secured the picture on my wall and stepped back to look at it, it suddenly looked lovely. The odd colors merged into a striking blend that depicts a wind-tossed sea and a sailboat moving calmly through the water.

In the same way, the elements God uses to create His perfect design in our lives may seem splattered haphazardly on our "canvas," but when we look at God's work with an eternal perspective, we see a beautiful plan of good for our lives. God knows the final picture He's painting. We need to wait in faith for the opportunity to step back and see His completed handiwork in our lives.

Right now, I know a family whose teenage son is seriously ill from cancer. Watching them walk through this valley day by day is extremely difficult. We pray for God's healing and wonder why this young man has to go through such pain. God's brushstrokes aren't very beautiful right now because we can't step back to view His finished picture. But by faith, even in the midst of seemingly unanswered prayer, we can trust that God's creative hand is at work. In time, the canvas of that family's life will be complete. Then God's sovereignty will be even more evident than it is right now. Keeping an eternal perspective helps us to trust God and be assured that He knows what He's doing, even when we may not appreciate the elements He is using to design our lives.

We've all been in situations where we wondered about God's creative purposes in unpleasant circumstances. My friend, Emily, recently had her doubts while substitute teaching in a high school. She e-mailed me about it saying, "I think if I have another week like this, I will be in the market for another job. It certainly has its challenges and I can look at it as a ministry, I suppose, but being abused, persecuted, and humiliated simply because I represent an authority figure does not provoke me to wake up in the morning looking forward to my day!

"But then I think . . . is God showing me something about entering into His sufferings? I think perhaps one of the hardest things Jesus endured was His loneliness and constantly being misunderstood even by His closest friends. Do you think, Kathy, that God puts us in positions sometimes where we feel some of that pain He felt so we can draw on God's strength and not our own? Or is the pain and discomfort an indication that we should move on and find something more palatable to our own joy and happiness? That's my question for this week!"

I related to Emily's comments. It's not always easy to discern what we're supposed to learn through suffering. But I'm convinced that when we keep our eternal glasses on, we will find it easier to appreciate whatever God allows. If we can see each challenge and trial as meant for our good, our growth, and His glory, we will be able to handle it better. We may not be able to jump up and down in joy over it all, but by believing through the eyes of faith that there is eternal purpose behind the problem, we will be able to rejoice, always.

About now, I can just imagine some of us saying, "Well, maybe I don't want God's brand of 'good' for me then. If it requires so much difficulty, then I'd rather go without, thank you very much!" We all feel like that at times. Many of us have lamented, "God said He wouldn't give me more than I can handle. Well, I wish He didn't think so highly of me!" But if we have an eternal perspective, we'll understand that God is preparing us for heaven.

When we're struggling on our way toward our heavenly home, we might be tempted, as the Israelites were, to hightail it back to a time when things seemed easier. After God's people were delivered from their captivity in Egypt and began their journey toward the Promised Land, their stomachs started to growl in the desert and they longed for the food they enjoyed in "the good old days." (I guess they forgot about the abuse they endured!) Like them, we may be tempted to sacrifice the character and hope God is hammering into our lives when our journey takes us into the desert.

At those times, it is helpful to reflect on what life was really like before we began to experience God's creative redemption. I can remember more than a few disadvantages of life before I let God take over. I was:

- constantly feeling guilty and couldn't find a means to discover peace.
- always dissatisfied with my progress.
- constantly evaluating whether I was good enough to make it into heaven.
- expecting too much from myself and others because I thought making life perfect would bring happiness.
- constantly thinking I would arrive at a point in time when problems wouldn't bother me—or when they would be eliminated all together.

That was no fun! Do I want to go back? No! Living in the center of God's will for my life may not eliminate problems, but it does provide the glorious assurance that everything in my life will be used for my good. When I see life through God's eyes, I recognize that my problems are the means to God's end: the development of my character, the opportunity to see God glorified, and the awakening knowledge of future joys in heaven. Expecting God to use my pain and hardships for those purposes assures me that God is in charge, even when life seems out of control.

God wants to use everything you and I go through. With your limited vision from earth, it may be difficult for you to imagine that He has a higher goal in your suffering, one that could even glorify Christ. Right now, in the midst of your pain, or because of confusing circumstances from the past, God's plan may seem very hazy. Perhaps you were abused as a child. Maybe your job is really putting you through the wringer. You may be struggling with a sin that seems to have you in a vise grip. Your body could be succumbing to an unwelcome disease. Possibly a friend you've always counted on is giving you the cold shoulder. Or you may fear you'll never know the reason for your suffering until you're in heaven. While you're in the midst of such trials, a higher good doesn't seem possible—or even of interest. But God knows His plan for your good and His glory, and He doesn't waste anything. In that you can rest in faith, and rejoice.

The Ultimate Good

Author Jennifer Maze Brown reminds us that the most powerful good we can experience here on earth is the one that makes us desire and value heaven all the more. Jennifer learned that after she lost three babies to miscarriage. She writes, "All were born only a few short weeks after their lives began, before onlookers could even tell they were there. But I knew. I already loved them."[3] Because there wasn't a memorial service, Jennifer and her family planted a miniature rose bush in the corner of their yard by the fence. Jennifer describes that time: "As we patted the soft soil around the little roots, we explained to our children that a rosebud sometimes may swell on this side of the fence, but if the stem grows through that barrier, it actually blooms on the other side. Our baby was like the little rose. He began here, but went on to live with Jesus before he 'bloomed'—before we could know him. That seemed to make sense to them, and soon, though they were disappointed, they were content to anticipate getting to know this brother or sister in heaven."[4]

But it wasn't so easy for Jennifer. She continued to grieve. "I knew my babies lived still, just on the other side. The other side was really there, and only a step away—just as heaven is. As God taught me to accept His will that I should live on this side for now and those babies on the other side, He birthed in my heart a new understanding of the reality of heaven."

Eventually, Jennifer's grief was diminished and she could reach out to others who were experiencing a similar loss and help them to appreciate the nearness of heaven. Jennifer knows the reality of heaven because of the grief she experienced. That was a powerful "good" that God deposited within her through what she suffered.

Rejoice in pain? Yes, God knows the plan. Rejoice when God's creativity seems to be producing something ugly? Yes, God knows what the finished masterpiece will look like. Rejoice when God seems to arrive late? Yes, God has a loving purpose. He can be trusted.

As you draw closer to God in the midst of suffering, you'll give Him glory. That's our theme for the next chapter. We'll continue to focus on facing life's challenges with an eternal perspective that counters the lie, "Life can't be enjoyed unless it's 'good' according to the world's definition." In reality, regardless of our condition or experiences, God can use us to display His glory and might. That truth enables us to live with a tremendous sense of purpose.

❧ *Questions* ❧

1. Why do you think Christians aren't spared from pain?

2. Think about a recent trial or difficulty you experienced. To what degree did you achieve an eternal perspective? What could you do differently next time in order to look at your suffering through God's eyes?

3. Review Martha and Mary's experience in John 11:1-44. Which sister do you relate to the most? How do you think you would have responded in that situation?

4. Can you think of a situation in your own life that parallels Mary and Martha's situation? How did God work in your circumstances? Is there a verse that became important to you during that time?

5. During what difficulty have you most seen the creativity and goodness of God? Write about the experience and the good that God brought out of it. Which of the qualities listed in Romans 5:3-5 were brought into your life?

6. Has God ever used your own sin to draw you closer to Him and bring good into your life? If so, how?

7. If you've shared your experiences with others, how have they been helped by what you've learned through your suffering?

8. What do you want your response to be the next time you experience some trial or problem?

9. What verse mentioned in this chapter would help you remember the purpose for experiencing grief, pain, or problems? Memorize that verse.

5

Purpose

My purpose is to glorify God
whether or not my life conforms to the
world's definition of "good."

Can you see how awesome it is to know that you have
been created for God's glory? That you are to live in
such a way as to give all of creation a correct opinion or
estimate of who God is?

KAY ARTHUR

Aim at heaven and you'll get earth thrown in.
Aim at earth and you'll get neither.

C. S. LEWIS

 $\mathcal{W}$ E DON'T KNOW HER NAME BUT SHE EXHIBITED AN EARTHLY PER-
spective. She's known as "Job's wife" and she had come to the end
of her rope. Life was far from good or enjoyable. Imagine what the
scene might have been like.

Job's wife is in her tent, the harsh wind blowing through the
open flap. Regardless of the heat, she wraps her clothes tighter
around her, as grief wraps its chill around her heart. *It's just too much.
What good is life? My children! My children!* A wail begins in her
chest, rising in her throat and escaping from her lips. *They're gone!
Forever gone!* Only this past week she had visited each one and
enjoyed their company. Now they were gone! She just knew her
heart would break into a thousand pieces. *Oh God, why all of them?
Couldn't You have at least spared one? Not all of them!*

Her lament is interrupted as Job hobbles into the tent. He can
barely walk. Grotesque boils and sores cover his whole body. His
own grief over the loss of their children and everything they owned
had been interrupted by this horrible disease that disfigured him
and caused constant pain. With each slow and agonizing step, he
moans. At the sight of him, his wife rises and goes to his side. "Job,
let me get some more of that salve the old woman recommended.
It's got to help some!"

Job looks up at her, his face bloated almost twice its normal
size. "Oh, wife," he says slowly through cracked lips, "nothing does
any good." He lowers himself painstakingly onto the rug and picks
up the broken pottery shard to begin his ritual of scraping the puss
off the open sores. The putrid smell permeates the room quickly.

"Oh, please," his wife cries out, "can't I do anything to help?
I've got to do something or I'll go crazy!"

Job looks up with compassion shining through his puffy eyes
in spite of his great pain. "I appreciate it, but there's nothing you

can do. We've just got to wait this out. I don't know what God's intentions are, but we must trust Him. I miss the children as much as you do, but somehow we'll see God's purposes revealed someday."

Job's wife had started to gently wipe one of his sores, but she suddenly throws the towel down. "God! God! I've had enough of hearing about God! If God is so wonderful, why did He allow all this to happen to us? And look at you. You're pitiful! The only way you're going to stop hurting is to give up and die. This is no way to live at all! Job, death would be better!" Her voice had started out energized by anger but by the time she stops, it is a raspy declaration of hopelessness.

Job sets the piece of pottery down and weakly reaches out to her, but she jerks her shoulder away. Her sobs erupt from deep within her being. "The children! The children! They're dead!"

Job sucks breath into his lungs, enough to reply, "Woman, don't speak like those who don't know God's goodness. God has always been wonderful to us. Now it's time for us to suffer. Only in everything God should be glorified."

Job's wife drops to the floor, holding her hands over her ears. Rocking back and forth she continues to moan, "Why? Why? Why?"

Tears come to my eyes as I think of the grief Job and his wife suffered. I cannot self-righteously criticize her when I haven't experienced such great loss. Her ten children were dead, everything they'd worked to achieve had been burned, stolen, or killed. And yet Job was able to keep an eternal perspective in spite of his great grief and physical pain.

It would seem that Job's wife was a part of his great restoration. In the last chapter of the book of Job, we read that God rewarded him for his faithfulness and he again was blessed with great wealth and ten more children. Was his wife the mother of those children? Did she repent from her earthly perspective as her grief was healed and God finally revealed Himself to Job? I hope so.

What the World Says

Job's wife's challenge—to view life from a heavenly perspective and see the value of glorifying God—seemed impossible to her in those days of grief. Most of us don't experience such extreme circumstances, but life can still challenge us. When life isn't happy and enjoyable, can we still desire to please and glorify God? That's the challenge.

As I talk with women across the United States and receive letters from those reading my books, there is a vast variety of situations that make us wonder how God can be glorified. A wife wants to please God but her husband is unsupportive, angry, and critical. She wonders how long she can put up with it. She tries to find a Christian counselor through her employer's medical insurance but no one is available. Her secular counselor tells her, "Get out of that marriage and find someone else who will meet your needs."

A single woman who has always wanted a husband wonders why God doesn't answer her prayer for her soul mate. She knows she's getting cynical and she hates it but she really thought God would answer her prayer "yes." Her friends don't help her attitude because they pressure her to date unbelievers and to get her sexual needs met through "playing around."

Another woman shared with me that she has been in constant pain for ten years. She is known for her strength but senses her condition wearing down her faith and trust in God. Can she continue to glorify God even as she sometimes doubts His goodness? When she went to one support group, the people there said, "Take whatever drugs are necessary to relieve it, even if they are illegal."

For all these women, the world's view tells them, "You don't deserve to have life be unhappy or dissatisfying. Do whatever it takes to make life 'good' again." But for a Christian who wants to please God and glorify Him through her choices, many of the alternatives the world offers can't be considered.

God's Viewpoint

As we learn to look at life through God's eyes, we discover that our lives can honor and glorify Him regardless of the situation or circumstances we're in—and that glorifying God is purpose enough for living. First Corinthians 10:31 says to "do everything for the glory of God" (TLB). Having the underlying desire to please and honor God will give life its supreme purpose and a firm foundation. When we have such a solid footing, whatever happens that brings pain, discomfort, or disappointment will not cause us to stumble in our faith and confidence. We'll know that we have a higher calling: to see God glorified.

The Hebrew definition of "glory" is to "give the correct opinion or estimate of." Therefore, author Kay Arthur says, "Your life is to be lived in such a way as to reflect Him, to show the world the character of God—His love, His peace, His mercy, His gentleness. You are to live for Him, to accomplish His will. To miss this purpose is to miss fulfillment. It is to have existed rather than to have lived."[1]

I have found that though many things in life bring joy—and I'm determined to appreciate and soak in every single one of them!—what brings the greatest spiritual pleasure is bringing glory to God. In those moments when I obey Him even though I'd rather be selfish, my joy is greatest. Or when I step out in faith even though I'm scared, my heart is most encouraged. Or when I see people drawn closer to Him even though I thought my efforts were futile, that is the happiest and most successful time in my spirit. There's a deep satisfaction in knowing God was lifted up and I was a part of it! Even though I don't always obey or risk or represent Him faultlessly, God's faithfulness takes my small steps and turns them into big steps for Him. When I take off the lenses of an earthly perspective that focus on my comfort and safety and put on God's heavenly glasses that encourage me to desire His glory and focus on Him, I'm thrilled and life has a higher degree of joy.

The apostle Paul experienced this. Even while imprisoned and suffering persecution, Paul had an eternal perspective that gave him a deep sense of purpose and joy. Listen to these words of magnificent confidence in Christ and His purposes through us on this earth:

> Now I want you to know, brothers, that what has happened to me has really served to advance the gospel. As a result, it has become clear throughout the whole palace guard and to everyone else that I am in chains for Christ. Because of my chains, most of the brothers in the Lord have been encouraged to speak the word of God more courageously and fearlessly. It is true that some preach Christ out of envy and rivalry, but others out of goodwill. The latter do so in love, knowing that I am put here for the defense of the gospel. The former preach Christ out of selfish ambition, not sincerely, supposing that they can stir up trouble for me while I am in chains. But what does it matter? The important thing is that in every way, whether from false motives or true, Christ is preached. And because of this I rejoice. Yes, and I will continue to rejoice, for I know that through your prayers and the help given by the Spirit of Jesus Christ, what has happened to me will turn out for my deliverance. I eagerly expect and hope that I will in no way be ashamed, but will have sufficient courage so that now as always Christ will be exalted in my body, whether by life or by death. For to me, to live is Christ and to die is gain. (Philippians 1:12-21)

That word "exalted" can also be translated "magnified." Kenneth S. Wuest, former Moody Bible Institute professor, writes, "The word 'magnify' is the translation of a Greek word meaning, 'to make great, to make conspicuous, to get glory and praise.' Paul's desire was that the Lord Jesus might be seen in his life in all His beauty, that He might be conspicuous, that He might get glory and praise to Himself through Paul."[2]

In Warren W. Wiersbe's book, *Be Joyful*, I found a delightful explanation of how we can envision "magnifying" Jesus through our own lives. Wiersbe writes, "Does Christ need to be magnified? After all, how can a mere human being ever magnify the Son of God? Well, the stars are much bigger than the telescope, and yet the telescope magnifies them and brings them closer. The believer's body is to be a telescope that brings Jesus Christ close to people. To the average person, Christ is a misty figure in history who lived centuries ago. But as the unsaved watch the believer go through a crisis, they can see Jesus magnified and brought so much closer."[3]

When you and I go through difficult situations, whether big or small, and we depend upon the Lord, Jesus will appear "bigger" in the eyes of others. They will recognize that our power comes from Him. Ephesians 2:10 assures us, "For we are God's workmanship, created in Christ Jesus to do good works, which God prepared in advance for us to do." We can be confident that if He plans the work for us to do, He will be faithful to bring the results He desires for His own glory. We only need to obey. God *will* be magnified and glorified! We just need to cooperate with Him so we'll be empowered to carry out the wonderful plans He has already designed.

My friend, Ruthie Swain, glorified God in powerful ways, even though she didn't know it at the time. As she lived victoriously through a severe trial, the Christian faith she had long professed was revealed in God-honoring ways.

When Ruthie's beloved husband, Perv, died unexpectedly at age fifty-one, her world was torn apart. Larry and I met this dynamic couple during the couples' retreat that God used to begin the healing of our marriage. They were one of the couples who shared their lives with us that weekend, and because of their love for each other, Larry and I were confronted with our own lack of love. After that we kept in touch with the Swains and were so sad to hear that Perv's life had ended on this earth.

Ruthie was suddenly an "oddball single" after being involved in couples' ministries for many years. She says, "I remember saying to God, 'I hate this school of experience, but, at least, please don't let me flunk.' If I had a goal, it was to survive my grief as a single, stay healthy for the sake of my two daughters, handle all the details of life, and stimulate my shocked brain with inspiring and funny material. Never did the thought cross my mind that I must glorify God in all this. But others who've observed my life through the last eighteen years since Perv died are inspired to realize that with God's help, one can survive victoriously. What God did for me brings Him glory. But it was still hard for me."

As I've considered the concept of glorifying God, I've realized that it's not so much what we do that brings glory to God, but the attitude we do it with—and who gets the credit for our perspective. There are many people who do wonderful things, yet they aren't motivated to give God credit or glory. People who are not Christians assist the poor at homeless shelters, give to charity, do volunteer work, give a dollar to the man holding a sign at the freeway entrance, and countless other good things. All these actions make our world a better place. But those people don't necessarily desire to have God glorified through their actions.

Even when Christians do good works, God may or may not be glorified. In order to receive glory through us, those watching must know we claim His name. Many people say that our lives are like a book that people can read and see God. I'm not so sure I agree with that premise if those watching don't know where we're getting our strength. Just living a good life, or dealing well with a difficult situation—without speaking of God—won't necessarily make people recognize His work and give glory to Him. Again, many people cope well with life, go through difficult situations in their own power, and never credit God. Just living well won't bring God honor unless our observers already know we're Christians or we say something about the Lord. That doesn't mean we'll speak of Him in every situation. God's perfect timing may require that we hold off temporarily. But we can't assume that people are seeing God in us if we've never told them He is the one who makes the difference.

I've discovered at least five ways that Christians can glorify God in daily life. One is by simply following His instructions. Sometimes glorifying God requires risk. God is often glorified when we rejoice in the midst of our difficulties, or when we respond to life from our highest self rather than from our sin nature. We are also called to glorify Him by standing up for righteousness and making right choices even when it's difficult. Let's examine each of these avenues to exalting God in more detail.

Obeying God's Instructions

Like Ruthie, when we obey God and have opportunities to tell how He empowered us to live for Him, that draws people's attention to Him. Obedience can be easier if we see the great purpose of bringing glory to Him. A supernatural joy overtakes us as we think, "Y'know what? If I obey God, He's going to get the credit! I'm going to do it!" The Word encourages us to "Declare his glory among the nations, his marvelous deeds among all peoples" (Psalm 96:3, NIV). We can do that as we cooperate with those already designed plans that Ephesians 2:10 talks about.

I experienced that some time ago while waiting in the airport for my connecting flight. I was minding my own business and reading my novel when I looked up and noticed a small food counter nearby where a woman was serving customers. As I continued reading, I felt an unexpected divine nudge. The Lord's still small voice within my heart whispered, "Go talk to that woman behind the counter about Me."

Unfortunately my first reaction was one I usually have: "Oh, Lord, you know I don't like doing things like this. Please! No!"

I could sense Him patiently waiting.

"Oh, all right, Lord. What should I say to her?"

"Tell her I love her."

Well, that wasn't very original! I still wasn't convinced I should go and I tried to distract myself with reading my book. But I knew God wouldn't let me rest so I gathered my things together and got in line at the counter. I was amazed that by the time all the customers in front of me had been helped, no one had gotten in line behind me.

When I faced the woman at the counter, I gulped and shot off an arrow prayer, "Okay, Lord, here we go." I spoke up. "Ma'am, I know this will sound strange, but God wanted me to tell you He loves you."

The woman's face seemed to harden for a second. "Oh, no, Father, what have you gotten me into now?" I cringed.

But then suddenly, her face softened and tears welled up in her eyes. She stared at me in surprise and said, "Oh, thank you. My husband recently died and I'd begun to believe God didn't love me. Thanks for telling me that."

I ordered my iced tea and she began sharing her hurt and pain with me. As I went to the side of the counter to mix in the sweetener, she followed me over and again thanked me for reaffirming her belief in God's great love. God had opened a door of opportunity and I was so glad I hadn't refused His prompting. In that small encounter, I knew that He had been glorified and I was thrilled to have the privilege of seeing His hand at work.

Whether or not we clearly hear God whispering instructions, we can glorify God by obeying His Word. For some women that will mean staying with an unsaved husband. Of course, God doesn't want any woman to be abused. But if she is feeling discouraged because her husband hasn't become a Christian and she dreams about having a spiritual leader, God doesn't want her to go seeking someone else. Staying faithful though all her needs aren't being met and attributing to God her ability to give her husband unconditional love will illuminate God's power in the sight of others. Unbelievers may not always agree but they will respect the strength it takes. And it may be that another Christian wife who is struggling to stay committed to her husband will be inspired to stay committed to her marriage during a difficult time.

Your obedience may take the form of doing something nice for neighbors even though they yell at your son when his football bounces into their yard. Greeting people with a cheerful "Good morning" as you walk around the park could draw someone into conversation. Any small act of kindness can glorify God as you obey His instructions, whether big or small.

Taking Risks

As you and I obey God in ways that seem unusual or seem to put us at risk, God can be glorified. Peggy Westerfeld has taken such a step recently. For over six years, she loved her job of coordinating seminars in the international department of a large Christian ministry. She was having a profound impact on encouraging Christians from around the world. She also loved coming home from work and sharing her exciting activities with her husband and three young sons. She was fulfilling her lifelong desire to be a missionary in a unique way.

But then the Lord seemed to be leading her to quit her job. She was surprised because she didn't want to leave her "ministry" or risk the lower income. But in obedience, after seeing God confirm her choice in many ways, Peggy left the full-time job and began working part time out of her home. She felt devastated. This wasn't fulfilling her dream to be a missionary! For several weeks, she felt sorry for herself. The only redeeming light was greeting her boys after school. They loved having her there, as she knew they would.

Recently, Peggy, her husband, Chuck, and their sons had done some extra upkeep on their rental property in a low-income area. The boys became acquainted with the children who lived in the neighborhood. Peggy saw the connection and felt God leading her to start an "After School Club" once a week. With the help of her sons, Peggy now leads thirty-five children in crafts and a spiritual object lesson each week. The mothers in the area are amazed that Peggy is doing this. She's having many opportunities to tell them about the God she loves.

The most unexpected result of the choices Peggy has made, however, came when she and Chuck told Chuck's father that Peggy quit her job. Chuck's father is an atheist and his initial attitude was, "You're crazy to give up the income." But once Peggy explained her motivations, he followed her into the kitchen and said, "I respect you for the decision you've made." Peggy was blown away! God had used her risky step of faith to honor Himself before a man they had been trying to witness to for many years.

Peggy's desire to follow God's leading at any cost has been worth it. Her joy in caring for her sons and seeing God provide for their financial needs has strengthened her faith and been a testimony of God's goodness to those around her.

What risk have you taken that has glorified God? You may not always be able to see the fruit, but God has used you more than you realize. It could be as simple as taking that plate of cookies over to your new neighbor's house, wondering how she will respond. Or it may be a more dramatic act, like my friend Lisa Ruby's. Lisa risked the criticism of others when she broke her marriage engagement to a young man. Some may have considered her foolish because he was a delightful person, but after she read Elisabeth Elliot's book *Passion and Purity*, she knew he wouldn't be the spiritual leader she wanted.

Lisa says, "I believe that God was glorified because some of my other friends decided to not settle for marrying just anyone, but hold out for the godly man they desired. I was fearful at first that I would let people down or that some would be disappointed in me, but I had to take the risk and obey God. A lot of people were shocked about what I did but when they heard why I broke off my engagement, they understood. I actually ended up gaining a lot of people's respect. I didn't know if that would happen or not."

Those around Lisa have seen God magnified through her willingness to risk criticism and the possible anger of that first young man. When we take risks as we follow God, our choices will bring Him glory as others see our willingness to do what God wants us to do regardless of the consequences.

Rejoicing During Hard Times

People who don't know the Lord may not always regard our obedience to God or even taking risks as important, but most people pay attention to someone who is able to rejoice in the midst of hard times. Our Christian friends may also be encouraged by our example.

I know I'm constantly inspired by God's obvious work in the life of my friend, Judy Snider. Judy has been bedridden from multiple sclerosis for fourteen years. I first met her and her husband, George, in 1978 when we were in a small group together. Larry and I enjoyed getting to know Judy's wonderful sense of humor and loving personality. But in time her physical problems increased and eventually in 1980 her doctors determined she had multiple sclerosis. The news was devastating to Judy and George and their three teenagers, but they hung in there and God strengthened them to cope.

Eventually, MS took away Judy's ability to walk and then to move. Today, she is completely bedridden and can only move her head. But she can still talk, smile, and communicate her trust and love for God, and that's what inspires so many.

From the world's standpoint—an earthly perspective—Judy doesn't have much of a life. What can she accomplish? What can she contribute to society? What hope does she have? Plenty! She would never brag about how God is glorified through her, but I will! Judy is an integral part of the food ministry at our church. She makes dozens of calls a week to coordinate a group of volunteers who deliver donated food to needy people in the community. "How can she do that if she can't even move her hands?" you might ask. Sometimes her husband dials for her, but she can also blow into a contraption connected to her phone to reach an operator, who will then dial for her because she's handicapped.

Judy explains how she became involved in this ministry. "I had read in our church's newsletter that they needed someone to make phone calls for the Food Fund, a program that gives donated food to needy families. At first I thought, 'They wouldn't want me.'

"But after I saw the announcement for the second week, I phoned and found out no one else had called. I've been doing it ever since and it builds my self-esteem. People say I take the time to talk to them. I'm glad the Lord has given me two ministries: calling for the Food Fund and praying for people. It makes me feel more content. I feel like I'm doing more than just lying here."

Not only does Judy reach out to strangers, but she also is a blessing to her family, especially her grandchildren. When many grandparents are off doing their own thing, having little time to invest in the lives of their grandchildren, Judy is always there for the five grandkids. She's the grandma who doesn't do other things when a child speaks. She's the grandma who listens with her ears and her eyes. She's the grandma who gives encouragement even when a child feels like a failure at school. Her love for the Lord is exemplified in her love for her grandchildren.

Several summers ago, a group of teenagers from our church helped out George and Judy by doing some yard work for them. During their lunch break, Judy invited the young people into her living room, where her bed was set up. As they ate their sack lunches near her bedside, they noticed the praise music she was listening to and her cheerful spirit. On the bus ride back to the church, some of the teens talked about Judy, her attitude and love for the Lord. They were struck by the intense faith she had in God despite her disability. A mother of one of the teens commented, "At least one person from that group will someday be dealing with a disability, and they will think back to that summer afternoon. Remembering Judy's faith will strengthen them to trust God for their own difficulty."

Judy's outreach and ministry of prayer and service blesses

many, both directly and indirectly. God is using her to bring glory to Himself. But more important than what she does is who she is. Judy has been a powerful example to me, over many years, of a person who lives for God. Her life exemplifies the truth of Psalm 105:2-3, "Sing to him, sing praise to him; tell of all his wonderful acts. Glory in his holy name; let the hearts of those who seek the LORD rejoice" (NIV).

You may not be facing anything as difficult as Judy is, but you can still glorify God by rejoicing in hard times. As you express your trust in God, even when life hurts or is disappointing, He will be magnified in the eyes of others. You can't force people to receive your words, but God will cause their hearts to respond through His Spirit working within them.

Responding in Godly Ways

Have you ever had someone say to you, "I sure didn't expect you to respond like that!"? If your response was a godly one in the face of insult or injury and the person observing you knows you're a Christian, it most likely caused him or her to credit God for your self-control. You may have treated someone nicely who has treated you with disdain. Or maybe you've been able to express appreciation or gratitude for something that is painful. Perhaps you've been the source of healing between two warring factions in your church or family—and no one had previously considered you a mediator type. Responding in God-honoring ways, against our natural inclinations, can magnify God in the sight of others.

My friend Kathryn is experiencing that right now. Her daughter's husband has just decided to continue his schooling after getting two master's degrees in engineering. Now he wants to start medical school! Her daughter has had enough and, for many other reasons as well, has left her husband. But Kathryn hasn't given up on her son-in-law. She wants to stay in dialogue with him with the hope that this marriage can be restored and he might become a Christian.

As a result, she calls and e-mails him on a weekly basis and expresses concern about his father's terminal illness. Her unconditional love hasn't always been understood by everyone, especially her unbelieving friends. But they acknowledge that God is giving her the power to do something they couldn't do. They respect her for it.

We can also give glory to God when we change our attitude or behavior because of His power at work within us. Have you previously been discouraged about being unemployed but now you're able to trust God? I'm sure your friends have noticed your new attitude and relaxed confidence. Maybe you've always been critical of your mother-in-law but lately you've expressed some appreciation to your friends and they've been amazed! You've even had an opportunity to tell how God has changed your attitude. That brings God glory. Or maybe you've always been the shy type and didn't want to help out at church functions. But now you're inviting your co-workers to the Mother-Daughter Tea because you're in charge of decorations. As you tell how God has empowered you to do something that's not your "cup of tea," they'll be curious about the God you serve. Or perhaps you're trying to find volunteers for your community recycling drive and no one seems to be responding. But you're not worried; you know the Lord will supply the people you need. Your peace and trust in God will cause the people around you to wonder whether they can trust Him too.

In big and small ways, God wants to appear "bigger" in the eyes of others because of your actions, responses, and attitudes. Whether your life is filled with happiness or difficulty, supportive people or critical people, excitement or the mundane, your responses will let people know that life doesn't have to be "good" in order for you to enjoy and appreciate it. In fact, the more you suffer and stay true to God, the more God will get the glory. With this perspective, life can be an exciting adventure. Can you catch the excitement? Can you look at what you're facing as an opportunity to magnify God in the eyes of others? God wants to empower you to do that.

If you've been trying to point others to God through the way you live, and yet you're discouraged because you aren't seeing any fruit, then trust the Lord for that too. I'm convinced that you and I are glorifying God in many ways we can't see. I saw an example of that a few months ago when I spoke for a national convention in Nashville. A woman approached me and explained, "Fourteen years ago I heard you speak at a woman's conference. I was told to go listen to you even though I wasn't married and didn't have children. You spoke about your experience of abusing your child and I couldn't relate. I sat there restless, judging you. But eventually, I married and had children. As I struggled with frustration toward them, I thought of you many times and your words helped me. Thank you for making a difference in my life!"

Making Righteous Choices

Recently in our local newspaper, a columnist profiled a man who found an envelope with a check for several hundred thousand dollars in it and turned it over to police so that the owner could be found. The columnist said that if he had found that money he would rationalize keeping it. He admired a person who would return it.

I was surprised at the columnist's honesty, but the world often has an earthly attitude: "Society owes me and if I just happen to find something that isn't mine, well . . . I deserve it." Yet that isn't the eternal perspective God wants us to have. He wants us to make right choices because He knows that as a result, He'll be glorified.

The apostle Peter writes in his first letter, "Live such good lives among the pagans that, though they accuse you of doing wrong, they may see your good deeds and glorify God on the day he visits us" (1 Peter 2:12, NIV). When you and I make right choices, those who don't know the Lord may not always think it's necessary, but they do respect it. And they expect it!

Several years ago, my sister, Karen Dye, made some unwise choices when she failed to pay all the taxes on the sales from her and her husband's restaurant. She wasn't a Christian at the time but, through the consequences of their losing everything and going into bankruptcy, she turned to the Lord. Now she glorifies God by claiming every cent and is very careful to be truthful in everything she does. She is able to magnify the Lord and give Him the credit because their new business is thriving and they have tenfold what they had in their previous location. I'm sure some of the people she deals with think that she's too picky about accounting practices, but they certainly can't say anything against Karen's success.

Karen also magnifies the Lord through her righteous attitudes. She and her husband's current restaurant is in a very small town and many new restaurants are threatening competition. When a hamburger chain recently built a new restaurant in town, Karen was fearful and angry. She thought, "What will it do to our business? Why can't they see there isn't room for a new enterprise?" In her fear, she wanted to complain and be negative as she dealt with other people in the community. But the Lord quickly got her attention and told her to bless the new business instead of complain about it. She certainly didn't feel like doing that but she realized it was the right thing to do.

Though many business people in town have had a negative response to the new restaurant, Karen is careful to keep a positive attitude. "Our sales this year have been down for the first time in the twelve years," she says. "But as I have glorified God by blessing that new restaurant, God has stretched those smaller sales and we've actually netted more this year than any previous year. He has taught me that He is my provider. Nothing, not even a rash of new restaurants, can take away His provision if He wants to bless us. I know God is providing abundantly for us now through our good choices, but I can't wait to see all the *eternal* consequences of our choice to glorify Him."

You may not always be aware of how the Lord uses your righteous choices to magnify His name. Maybe others have been inspired to consider God's righteousness when you asked someone's forgiveness for a wrong choice you made, or you drove in heavy traffic without cursing the person who cut you off. You might have glorified God through telling someone about a sin you struggle with and asking her to pray—even if she's not a Christian. Being vulnerable often impresses someone more than trying to be perfect.

You and I just never know what God is doing. I love the promise of Isaiah 25:1: "O LORD, Thou art my God; I will exalt Thee, I will give thanks to Thy name; For Thou hast worked wonders, Plans formed long ago, with perfect faithfulness." He is using you for His glory and He'll continue to do that through those plans He's already designed. Just put on your heavenly glasses, keep your focus on the Lord, and look for those opportunities to fulfill His purpose. As He leads you, your joy and excitement will increase.

In the next chapter we'll examine how to have an eternal perspective that helps us choose to be a servant, even when we want to be selfish and protect our resources. It is often hardest to keep a heavenly viewpoint when we're afraid of losing something by giving of ourselves.

❧ *Questions* ❧

1. Read the account of Job's losses in Job 1–2:10. In what ways do you relate to Job's wife's struggle?

2. How do you see the earthly view of "Life isn't enjoyable unless it's good" expressed in the world around you?

3. In what ways do you sometimes succumb to the world's philosophy? In what specific ways have you refused to agree with it?

4. Review 1 Corinthians 10:31. Can you think of anything that doesn't have the potential of being used for God's glory? How does this verse give you purpose for living?

5. Read again Philippians 1:12-21. What strikes you most about Paul's attitude? In what ways is your own attitude similar to Paul's or different from it?

6. In what way(s) have you seen God "exalted" or "magnified" in your life (Philippians 1:20)? How did it make you feel to be used by Him? How did it give your life more purpose?

7. Do you know someone who experiences an ongoing struggle of some kind, yet exhibits a desire to glorify God? What do you appreciate most about his or her attitude? If you have the opportunity, ask him or her how he or she sustains such a perspective.

8. Of the five ways suggested for achieving our purpose of glorifying God (obeying His instructions, taking risks, rejoicing in hard times, responding in godly ways, making righteous choices) which are easiest for you and which are hardest? Explain why for each.

9. What plan can you make to glorify God in one of the "hard ways" this week?

10. Meditate on Philippians 1:12-21 and ask the Lord to help you have the kind of heavenly perspective the apostle Paul did. In the week ahead, write down the ways God answers your prayer.

6

Service

I can be a living sacrifice
because God will take care of me.

Service takes us through the many little deaths of going
beyond ourselves.

RICHARD J. FOSTER

If you read history you will find that the Christians who
did most for the present world were precisely those who
thought most of the next. It is since Christians have
largely ceased to think of the other world that they have
become so ineffective in this.

C. S. LEWIS

E HAD A GREAT TIME THAT WEEKEND! THE GIRLS' CLUB THAT I belonged to as a teenager was lots of fun and our annual weekend in the mountains was especially great. We played games, ate, threw snowballs, ate, fixed each other's hair, ate, and sang songs around the fireplace. The adults—our parents—treated us like princesses. Although we each had one time of KP, the adults primarily did everything in the kitchen: fixing food and cleaning up. What could be better than having fun with little work involved?

On Sunday before we left, during our final time around the fireplace, the excitement continued as thanks were expressed and awards given—all in fun. But then one of the awards had a serious nature. Our adult emcee announced that a special award was being given for the first time for the girl who had sacrificially helped out in the kitchen without being asked. The moms who worked there had appreciated it and so they wanted to honor her. Suzi was called to the front and given a homemade ribbon labeled "Best Servant."

As soon as the award was given, my first thought was, "Well, if they'd let me know there was going to be an award, I would have helped out too."

OUCH! I immediately saw my attitude for what it was: selfish. I was willing to sacrifice and serve—if it was noticed and awarded. That, of course, wasn't being a servant at all! I clapped all the louder for Suzi, recognizing her selflessness and my lack of it.

Selfishness and selflessness. Touchy topics . . . especially for women. Most women spend plenty of time serving others. Unless they have a husband who is willing to help around the house, they are the ones who are working from morning to night—often outside the home as well as inside. But having a servant's heart is still something we need to address because it's so crucial to living with an eternal perspective.

The world would like us to believe we need to "look out for number one." We're encouraged as a society to do our own thing, regardless of the cost to others. The media and feminists encourage women to do whatever is best for them—even if it means hurting others. In addition, an earthly perspective can whisper in our souls, "If I sacrifice, I'll be taken advantage of." We're afraid we'll be mistreated. If a woman is a servant to her husband by cooperating with his plans, she may fear he'll expect her to "submit" without ever asking for her opinion. If she's selfless at church, she may be afraid she'll be called on to do everything and end up burning out. If she's selfless with her grown children, she might suspect they'll expect her to babysit the grandchildren without taking in account her own activities. We're afraid that if we're selfless, people won't say "thanks;" they'll think they can expect us to sacrifice all the time.

One woman shared with me her fear of becoming like her mother, who seemed to truly be taken advantage of. Her mother always ate the burnt piece of food so her family could have the rest. She rarely bought anything for herself even though there was sufficient money. She cooked her own birthday dinner and said, "Oh, it doesn't matter." My friend said, "My mother's pattern of being a martyr and sometimes a victim caused the family to take advantage of her generosity. She should have stood up for herself sometimes and modeled for us a strong, confident Christian woman who can set boundaries. Unfortunately, she still hasn't learned. My father continues to expect her to cook him lunch every day at noon, regardless of her plans."

That example of "selflessness" is often the idea we carry, but that isn't God's model or desire for us. If we misinterpret being a servant as meaning we must give all we have, then when we burn out and have nothing left to give we'll be confused and disheartened. We'll wonder why God didn't honor our sacrifice.

That may be what happened to Jackie. Jackie is a Christian woman who, from all appearances, was the epitome of a selfless servant of God. Yet she never saw how an earthly perspective began to creep into her thinking and reacting. She was a pastor's wife in a poor area of Los Angeles and her husband's salary was minimal. Both of them worked other jobs to support themselves and their two children. They were working hard for the Lord and in the early days they loved each other, their family, and God. Their sacrifice was clearly evident.

One day Jackie's mother noticed that Jackie was wearing scuffed and tattered sandals, even though it was the cold, rainy season. "Honey, why aren't you wearing some better shoes?" her mother asked.

Jackie rolled her eyes. "Because, Mom, I don't have any other shoes."

Her mother went right out and bought her a pair of shoes, but unfortunately, the emptiness of her soul and spirit could not be so easily corrected. In time, Jackie's life of service caused her to begin feeling sorry for herself. Soon, a man at work paid more attention to her than her husband did, and she transferred her affection to him. She left her husband and children, her husband lost his pastorate, and they were divorced.

In the beginning Jackie's heart was pure in her service for the Lord. Her selflessness was not fake. But because she didn't guard her heart and keep her motives pure, she began to slide into selfishness because she believed some of the earthly lies that said, "You shouldn't have to go without" and "If your husband doesn't love you the way you want, find someone who will." Overworked and underappreciated, Jackie succumbed to those lies.

We hurt with women like Jackie whose heartache leads them to make unwise and sinful choices. We hurt with those who have been abused by men and even the church as they strive to be selfless. Many women consider themselves inferior because they think of themselves as slaves—valuable only in their usefulness to others. Like Jackie, they consistently give more of themselves than they have available and end up hating themselves when they can't give more.

When my daughter was a toddler and my son was an infant,

I felt completely drained by their demands. I was grateful that I could stay home with them, but sometimes I believed that working outside the home would be easier. Each day the hours would go by and yet at dinnertime, exhausted and impatient, I couldn't think of one constructive thing I'd done. I'd actually done a lot but nothing seemed significant. Changing diapers, feeding a child who spilled milk constantly, mopping a floor that got dirty only minutes later, didn't seem significant. And then Larry would arrive home from work and ask, "What have you done today?" as he looked at the toys scattered across the family room floor. My own insecurities would rise up to fuel my shouted retort: "What do you mean, 'What have I done?' I haven't had a moment to myself!" But I couldn't think of anything either, and that made me even more angry!

In spite of how busy I was, I wondered whether I was being a true servant of God. I wasn't a missionary, hacking my way through the jungle to take the gospel to people who hadn't heard the name of Jesus. I wasn't like my pastor's wife who led women's ministries and sang in the choir. (I didn't know that she wasn't feeling good about herself either!) In my thinking, service and selflessness meant serving God actively in a way that brought glory to Him. In contrast, taking care of two kids and a husband just didn't seem to be included in the definition.

Now I know that I was truly serving the Lord by meeting the needs of the family God had given me. But biblical servanthood is still an elusive concept to define. I do know what it's *not*. It's not being a victim. It's not being a martyr. It's not false humility or having low self esteem. It's not having a slave mentality or being abused by a husband in the name of "submission." God values you and me as His children. We are His daughters in His royal court with a wonderful spiritual inheritance. Just as we can't imagine a princess being mistreated in the royal court, we can be sure that God doesn't want us mistreated. So how can we understand Christian servanthood in a way that inspires and strengthens us to glorify Him?

A Biblical Definition

First, Romans 12:1-2 exhorts us to see selflessness as God sees it: as worship! "Therefore, I urge you, brothers, in view of God's mercy, to offer your bodies as living sacrifices, holy and pleasing to God— this is your spiritual act of worship. Do not conform any longer to the pattern of this world, but be transformed by the renewing of your mind. Then you will be able to test and approve what God's will is—his good, pleasing and perfect will" (NIV). When we die to our selfish desires and surrender to obeying God when He calls us to serve, we are doing something holy and pleasing to Him. It's an actual act of worshiping Him.

Scripture gives us several examples of what it means to be selfless for the glory of God. First, Jesus' example in the garden of Gethsemane is a picture of the kind of selflessness God asks for. Jesus prayed, "Not my will, but yours be done" (Luke 22:42). That's biblical selflessness. It's submitting to the Father's will, doing what He wants us to do, while believing He has a beautiful plan even when we are called to sacrifice.

Bonnie is an example of Jesus' selflessness in the garden. When her son was born twenty-nine years ago with Down's Syndrome, such children were typically institutionalized. Though her doctors strongly suggested such a course, Bonnie believed God's will was taking Jonathan home, caring for him, and helping him achieve whatever level of accomplishment God wanted for him. The doctors said he wouldn't live long and would never walk or talk; he'd be "no more than a vegetable," they said.

But Bonnie's desire to fulfill God's plan has proved them wrong. Today Jonathan is a wonderful Christian man who loves God, graduated from high school, reads the Bible diligently, quotes Scripture, prays, and loves to serve others. When Bonnie said, "Not my will but Yours, Lord," God rewarded her service with a son who is a delight to everyone.

Although serving God and others isn't always easy and we can't be guaranteed that we'll see wonderful results as Bonnie did, we can be assured that if God has directed us to be selfless in some way, He's in charge of the results.

A second verse that gives us insight into true selflessness is 2 Corinthians 9:7: "Each man should give what he has decided in his heart to give, not reluctantly or under compulsion, for God loves a cheerful giver" (NIV). Although this verse is written about the giving of our finances, it is an overall principle in God's kingdom. Whether we give money, time, or love, God wants us to give cheerfully—not under compulsion or with a sour attitude.

My friend Constance shared with me about a time her friend called, wanting to come over to talk about her problems. Constance said, "I'd love to do that but I can only spare an hour because of my scheduled work." Her friend arrived and ended up spending five hours at her house. At first, Constance felt panicky and angry at her Christian sister's insensitivity. She was trying to figure out how to conclude their time. But then the Lord seemed to whisper, "I'm in charge of your schedule, just trust Me and minister to my hurting daughter." Her attitude changed, she could counsel her friend with wisdom and love, and her friend told her how much she was helped by their time together. Somehow, Constance's work got done speedily the next day and she was glad that she had given with a cheerful heart instead of grudgingly.

A third principle of selfless giving is found in Philippians 2:3-4: "Do nothing out of selfish ambition or vain conceit, but in humility consider others better than yourselves. Each of you should look not only to your own interests, but also to the interests of others"(NIV). *The Living Bible* expresses it this way: "Don't be selfish; don't live to make a good impression on others. Be humble, thinking of others as better than yourself. Don't just think about your own affairs, but be interested in others, too, and in what they are doing."

Those verses let us know that true selflessness is expressed by an attitude of humility and is devoid of ambition about its own promotion. It looks both to its own needs and to those of others, but is willing to put others ahead of itself. These verses don't say, "Don't meet your own needs." If we believe that warped view of "Christian" selflessness, we'll drain ourselves through sacrifice and never have anything to give. That's not God's will. Instead, He instructs us to take care of others *and* ourselves.

Jesus said, "Love your neighbor as yourself" (Matthew 22:39, NIV). He didn't say love others and hate yourself. In order to meet the needs of others, we must make sure our own needs are met. It's out of our own full souls that we'll be able to give sacrificially. Selflessness doesn't mean pouring ourselves out until we're bone dry; it means keeping ourselves filled up so that we can give abundantly to others.

Get Filled Up

That was author Gary Thomas's message some time ago when I heard him at a conference. Gary explains the difference between responding to people with a full soul and an empty one.

He gives a scenario when you haven't eaten for thirty-six hours and you've been invited to a great feast. When you arrive, the host explains that he needs your help serving the food. But you're starving. You agree anyway. As you serve the food, you angrily plop the food down on the tray, disgruntled that others get to eat when you can't. If someone complains about the food, you impatiently tell them to eat it anyway. By the time you can eat, you can't even enjoy it because you're so upset.

But if you are invited to that noon-time feast but attend a brunch before it, you arrive at the feast full. When the host asks you to serve the food, you cheerfully agree and don't mind waiting at all for your turn. You are courteous and kind to those who complain, and you attempt to meet their needs. A smile is firmly attached to your face and it's easy for you to wait for your turn.

The empty soul hasn't received God's love, presence, and grace. The full soul has already feasted on God's encouragement and love, the fellowship of the Spirit, and the support of others. That soul is now able to respond to others with joy, grace, and cheerfulness.

God cares about our needs and He wants them to be met. How does that happen? It must begin with our own relationship with Him. He is the source of our happiness, contentment, and ability to love others. Without a friendship with God that assures me I'm unconditionally loved and valued, I will never have the inner power or strength to sacrifice and be selfless. For me, my daily time alone with God is essential. An hour a day with God keeps my selfishness away—at least to some degree.

But I don't have an hour a day to spend with God! you might be thinking. I know that can seem especially true for mothers of young children. My children are young adults now so I don't have little ones interrupting my precious times with God. You may not yet have that privilege. You may set your alarm to have your devotional time before the children wake up and it always seems like they wake up early too. As soon as you're settled in the easy chair with your Bible, little padded feet are soon standing beside you, wanting breakfast. It seems impossible to get up any earlier, and even if you do, those padded feet are attached to a radar in your child's brain that says, "Mommy is awake. I'll go see her."

If this sounds familiar, try setting a snack beside you in the easy chair and offer it to your child so that you can delay breakfast. Include your child in your devotions. No, it won't seem as deep, but you'll be developing an important habit in your child's life. Another possibility is to arrange with another young mom to care for your child so that you can have time alone with God. You can return the favor. Or use a Mom's Day Out program in your community. Do whatever it takes to make time with God. That's not being selfish. You can't survive, much less serve sacrificially, without first getting your needs met by your Father in heaven.

Finding a Balance

Of course, selflessness doesn't always feel good. Joseph Stowell comments, "As we race toward the close of the twentieth century, most of the emphasis in Christianity is on becoming happier here, healed here, more blessed here, and more fulfilled here. Worship must excite our spirits, sermons must entertain and enthrall our minds, music must penetrate and propel us. And our counseling must make us feel better about ourselves and strengthen our human bond of friendship and family. While this may be nice and necessary, without heaven in clear view our Christianity fails to have a heavenward compulsion pulling us closer to God, closer to eternity, closer to home. It tends to become instead self-serving entertainment or a therapeutic center. A heavenless church seeks to satisfy longings and needs here rather than serving and sacrificing here with a view to satisfaction there.

"Without an eternal transcendent God as our compelling force and heaven in clear view, self becomes the center of attention and increasingly the center of our universe."[1]

Stowell is right, but as we seek an eternal perspective on the kind of sacrifice God asks of us, we must aim for balance. In order to continue to fill our own souls so we can serve others, we must be wise and discerning in responding to the demands of our family, our friends, our employers, our ministries. Selflessness doesn't mean we never stand up for ourselves or set reasonable boundaries. We are not at the mercy of everyone who desires our time, efforts, or money.

As always, Jesus is our example. In Luke 5:15-16, He demonstrates the balancing act of obeying God yet not being controlled by others: "But the news about Him (Jesus) was spreading even farther, and great multitudes were gathering to hear Him and to be healed of their sicknesses. But He Himself would often slip away to the wilderness and pray."

If Jesus had wanted to set an example of selflessness by doing everything everyone wanted, He wouldn't have left that needy group behind. They wanted Him to stay with them and meet all their needs. Instead, He needed to spend time with the Father—and He did. I can just imagine their disgruntled comments as He walked away. "Oh, He says He's the Messiah, huh? Well, if He is, why isn't He healing me? Why isn't He showing His power to me? He must not be any kind of God at all." But Jesus was not swayed by their needs, opinions, or demands. In fact, Jesus never responded to human need: He responded to what He saw His Father doing. Although He obviously felt compassion for all people, He didn't respond automatically; He responded out of obedience to God.

Jean Fleming writes, "Jesus did not heal everyone. He did not meet the needs of all the poor, or cast out all demons. I cannot meet every need I'm aware of. I cannot exploit every opportunity. . . . The goal of much that is written about life management is to enable us to do more in less time. But is this necessarily a desirable goal? Perhaps we need to get less done, but the right things."[2]

That is why I so often remind others, "An opportunity is not necessarily God's open door." Just because we hear of a need, though it may seem that we need to be selfless, it doesn't necessarily mean God wants us to respond. As Jesus listened intently to the voice of His Father and knew what His Father wanted Him to do, we must seek God's direction and only do what He wants us to do, regardless of what others think of us.

You and I face a great challenge when we try to hear and know what service God wants us to do. Our own mixed motives and wrong ideas can make it difficult to be sure. We must recognize our tendency to justify our selfishness, as well as our habits of feeling responsible for the choices and decisions of others.

Hilary, whose father's alcoholism took center stage while she was growing up, became her mother's confidante and defender. Later, Hilary married a man who became addicted to drugs and she fell into the same pattern of rescuing him by making excuses for his behavior. When she became a Christian, she turned those unhealthy responses into "Christian service," never being able to turn down any requests.

Now, through a codependency class at her church, Hilary is learning that it's Okay for her to say "no." She has made a commitment to pray before responding to any request and, as a result, when asked to take on a responsibility, she always says, "I'm so glad

you thought of me. I'll be glad to pray about it and get back to you."
Some people haven't appreciated her response, but one woman
thanked her because it modeled that *she* didn't have to say "yes"
immediately to everything either.

Hilary's example is one we need to pay attention to as we make
choices about our own service. We need to know when to say "no."
As we try to determine if we're being called to a responsibility or
ministry, we should also ask ourselves:

- Is this the best fit for me?
- Does this go along with my spiritual gifts?
- If I take this on, what steps will it take and how long will
  each step take?
- Do I feel pressured to do this just because it makes me
  feel important or needed?
- Am I seeking someone's approval or appreciation by
  saying yes?
- How will I feel if I do it and no one gives me credit?
- Have I asked for counsel from godly Christians who
  know me well?

These questions can help us to know God's will, and if He says
"yes," then they may also help us to keep a servant's attitude as we
obey Him. Selflessness doesn't care what role it plays as long as
God's plan is carried out.

The Benefits of Selflessness

As we carry out God's plan by serving Him and others in love, we
experience the ultimate benefit: being conformed to the image of
Jesus. Sacrifice results in Christlikeness, which is the ultimate goal
and privilege of every Christian.

My friend Bonnie Jeffers grew in her faith and dependence upon
God because of a time in her life that required her to be sacrificial.
When God called her husband, Jim, to be an assistant pastor in Lake

Arrowhead, California, she felt like she was in prison. She felt chained by all the expectations of being a pastor's wife. One church leader even told her that she drove too fast for a pastor's wife. She felt stifled by the lack of career opportunities in their small town. Without her friends, her old church, or a ministry she could call her own, she felt captive within the walls of her home. Every tree in her lovely mountain community seemed to be another prison bar around her.

"I wish I could say that I turned to the Lord for my strength," Bonnie says. "I didn't. I cried to my husband and yelled at God. The Lord has been part of my family's life for generations and has been my personal Savior since age six. But for the first time in my life, I found myself doubting God's love and even His existence. I wondered if I had been brainwashed since childhood by just another cult. In short, I went through a crisis of faith.

"During this time, however, Christ proved faithful even when I was faithless. He took me through it. He made me see that my belief in His existence from Sunday school and Bible college could survive in practice, not just in the classroom."

Like Bonnie, you may feel like you have prison bars around you at times. As you're called upon to be selfless, you may doubt that you can ever make your way through life's demanding terrain, much less gain something from the journey. But God is aware of your giving, and He is transforming you into His image as you sacrifice for Him. In your service, you are learning self-control and that builds your self-esteem. God is building you up, even when it's not in the ways you think you need.

My friend Melanie Hubbard shared an experience with me that communicates the truth that God is at work, even if we can believe that only by faith. "This summer while traveling in Utah," Melanie said, "we stopped along the Fremont River to swim at a delightful spot right at the base of a waterfall. After a while my husband and two children climbed up to the top of the falls and I stayed down below. When they reached the top, they all exclaimed about the beautiful rainbow they could see. I stood at the bottom and looked at the exact same spot but saw no rainbow. I knew they simply could see something beautiful that I could not. I just had to believe them that it really was there."

God is growing the fruit of righteousness in you. You may not see it and others may not acknowledge it, but it's there. Ask the Lord to show it to you.

Sacrificing with Purpose

Another glorious result of our service is sometimes the salvation of the lost and the sanctification of the saved. My friend Darren Prince is an example to me of sacrificing for God so that others will be loved into the kingdom. Darren is a twenty-three-year-old college graduate and the son of our friends, Dan and Judy Prince. He left a comfortable home to minister to the youth in San Francisco through the InnerCHANGE ministry. In his Christmas letter, he wrote of the sacrifices he has faced in trying to get settled: "The past two months have been some of the most inconvenient, frustrating, and humbling times of my life. You may already know that I've spent the majority of my first eight weeks in San Francisco just trying to find a place to live. After several seeming possibilities, much street pounding, and too many moves to count, I find myself still surrounded by those same travel-weary boxes I packed up back in May. . . .

"But I choose to see that God has had me on a special kind of 'identification' curriculum. At one level, I have felt the same sense of desperation and lack of options as many of my neighbors. One side effect of poverty is the inability to plan for the future with any sense of certainty—wondering what 'tomorrow' will look like."

Darren goes on to mention some of the victories he experienced, like ministry to a room full of teens, some of whom have requested personal visits. He has unloaded trucks full of donated clothing alongside young guys with huge, multicolored tattoos, multiple piercings, and torn-up jeans. "My job is to help get the job done while bringing the presence of Christ into their often dark worlds. This is a gigantic 'foot-in-the-door' for building relationships on the street as I see my 'coworkers' around the neighborhood all the time. . . .

"My human ambitions (and type-A personality) want to be able to report that I've seen tons of fruit harvested because of your prayer and support. But the real harvest thus far has been in my own heart. Through what we are tempted to call 'inconvenience,' 'setback,' and 'frustration,' He is cultivating the fruit of His Spirit."

Darren's example inspires me to be willing to sacrifice — even when it hurts. But I'm not the only one Darren's life has impacted. His mother, Judy, shared with me that God has used her son in her own life. When Darren felt God leading him into service in a dangerous location, she was naturally afraid. How could she release him possibly to put his life in danger — even for the Lord? Yet, the Lord was calling upon her to be selfless — to release her son and give up her own expectations of how her son's life should be run by God.

As she prayed, God led Judy to the truth of Acts 5:34-39. She saw His message to her in the verses, "If this plan or action should be of men, it will be overthrown; but if it is of God, you will not be able to overthrow it or else you may even be found fighting against God" (Acts 5:38-39). Judy says, "I didn't want to fight against God! I found that by depending on God to work out His plan in Darren's life, I could have peace to release him. If it were a desire of Darren's, without being the will or plan of God, to be in San Francisco, then it would be 'overthrown' anyway. God's plan is always good and I can trust Him even with the life of my firstborn."

Judy's selflessness required a release of her desire to safeguard her son's life. Now she is seeing the fruit of God's plan in great ways. Darren has become a mighty representative of the Lord and a mature Christian at a young age. She is amazed at Darren's Christian growth and dependence upon God. How could she not want that for him?

It certainly is what all Christian parents want for their children. God has brought glorious results out of Judy's purposeful sacrifice—both in her life and in her son's. In God's economy, our sacrifices will not be wasted or forgotten. Every deed done in His name is as if we were doing it to—and for—Him.

Sacrifice Is a Choice

Judy had to make a conscious decision to sacrifice, and it's the same for you and me. Someone has said, "The real test of servanthood is when you're treated like one." At those times, it's a decision of our will to choose selflessness—because we sure aren't going to feel like it. But if we do it anyway, God will bless our selflessness.

Penny Carlevato tells of the time that as a nurse she prayed to be able to minister on Jesus' behalf to her patients. One patient in particular had consistently resisted her efforts. On this particular night as she entered Donald's room, she prayed that his heart would be opened. She feared he could die soon, even though he was only in his late twenties. He was barely able to breathe, and after giving him his medications, Penny asked him how she could help make him more comfortable. He asked her to rub his back because it hurt so much.

She says, "As I carefully rubbed lotion on his back, I began to pray for him, and asked God again for the right words. But no words came. I closed my eyes and focused on Jesus as I continued gently massaging his fragile back. Donald seemed to be relaxing a little, his breathing quieter and slower. A feeling of peacefulness invaded the room.

"I opened my eyes, and instead of Donald in the bed, there sat Jesus! I closed my eyes quickly. I must be mistaken! I peeked again—yes, it is Jesus! I kept rubbing the back of Jesus and a feeling of perfect peace invaded the room. Then very slowly, Donald appeared back in his bed. By now, he had fallen asleep and I quietly left the room.

"'Oh, thank you, Jesus,' I prayed. 'I don't know how it happened that I saw You, I just know I did!' I realized in that moment that when we are available and willing to serve others, we are truly ministering to Jesus."

If we can remember the truth that Penny discovered, we'll be more empowered to sacrifice, for we're representing Him. You may witness for Him—often without even knowing it—by taking a meal to a grieving family in the neighborhood. You might be calling attention to Him as you patiently wait for the elderly woman in front of you in the check-out line while she searches for all her coupons in the bottom of her purse. You never know who is observing your attitude. It could be the very person you've been trying to lead to Christ. Without your knowing it, they could be watching you at the gym, department store, work, or while driving in your car. You and I are presented with choices every day: Will we choose to sacrifice in humility and love?

In March 1995, I happened to spot the newspaper obituary of a man who went around the world speaking of another man's selflessness. The headline read, "Franciszek Gajowniczek, 94; Auschwitz Survivor." I recognized the name because I had written about him in a previous book. Back in July 1941, Gajowniczek was a prisoner in Auschwitz and was randomly chosen to die along with nine prisoners as punishment for the escape of another prisoner. But as he pleaded for his life, saying he did not want to leave his wife and two sons, another prisoner stepped forward. Rev. Maximilian Kolbe, a Franciscan monk, bravely approached the commandant. Unexpectedly, the guards did not rush forward to beat him for his boldness.

"I have no family, but this man does," he told the officer in charge. "I want to take his place." The commander was briefly silent and then agreed, another unusual response.

Even though all ten prisoners were denied food and water, Kolbe survived longer than the other nine. Finally, the Nazis ended Kolbe's life in August 1941, with a lethal injection into his heart.

Gajowniczek was freed at the end of the war, returned to his family, and traveled throughout Europe and America, speaking of a monk who sacrificed his life. Kolbe gave him the selfless gift of fifty-four years.

You and I most likely won't be presented with an opportunity to die in someone's place, but daily we are challenged to be self-less by giving of ourselves for the glory of God. In whatever sacrifices we make, if we are serving because Jesus wants us to, we know God is pleased and we're honoring Him.

In our next chapter, we'll look at something that's closely related to sacrificial living: humility. What does that concept really mean and how can we live it out—when we're so wonderful! That's our next challenge in seeing life through God's eyes.

⇌ *Questions* ⇌

1. When you make a selfish choice, what usually motivates you?

2. When you choose to be selfless, what inspires you? When was the last time you were selfless, even in a small way?

3. Review Romans 12:1-2. How have you seen selflessness as a form of worship in your own life or in someone else's?

4. Consider again 2 Corinthians 9:7. How does a person who is "selfless" but not cheerful come across? How does his or her "sacrifice" make other people feel?

5. On page 102, Gary Thomas gives an example of the difference between a hungry soul and a full one. What do you do to feed your soul? What more would you like to do?

6. Do you have a hard or easy time saying "no" to requests you're convinced God doesn't want you to take? If so, why?

7. How does following Philippians 2:3-4 along with Matthew 22:39 help us achieve the balance of being selfless while meeting our own needs?

8. What will you tell yourself the next time you're tempted to say "yes" when you shouldn't?

9. Review the quote, "The real test of servanthood is when you're treated like one." When was the last time you experienced the test of being treated like a servant? What was your response?

10. If you passed the test, how were you able to do that? If you failed, what would you do differently the next time?

11. In what practical way do you anticipate you could be selfless within the next week? Ask the Lord to empower you for that occasion. And then thank Him in faith!

Humility

*I can choose humility and
boast in the Lord.*

What will it profit a man if he gains his cause, and
silences his adversary, if at the same time he loses that
humble tender frame of spirit in which the Lord delights,
and to which the promise of his presence is made!

JOHN NEWTON

There is always that one telltale sign when pride takes
charge: the fun leaves.

CHARLES SWINDOLL

$\mathcal{G}$ HAD MET A WOMAN AT A SUNDAY SCHOOL CONVENTION WHO WAS director of Women's Ministries for a church in a distant state. I hoped she would invite me to speak at her women's retreat. As we sat in the lounge of the convention center bouncing around ideas about ministering to women, I enjoyed one of the freshly baked chocolate chip cookies that had been provided. Unbeknownst to me, the soft chocolate of the cookie had dribbled down my lip and chin. When my new acquaintance inquired about my opinion on some important issues, I felt my "authoritative" voice take over. (I always later regret my intensity when that happens, but it seems to take over without my permission.) As I spoke with forceful and confident tones, I was thrilled to see my friend leaning forward, intently listening to my every word. Surely I was impressing her with my important comments! Surely she would be compelled to invite me to speak at her women's retreat.

In time, we made our way to the company booth to say our good-byes because the convention was concluding. Someone in her group suggested they take pictures and we huddled for a group picture, my security intact in being accepted into this group of important Christians. We hugged all around and said our fond farewells.

Before I left the conference center, I walked to the restroom, strolling along confidently, knowing the Lord had opened a door for future ministry. Our interaction had been mutually uplifting and my responses thoughtful and commanding. It had been a wonderful time.

I walked through the door of the rest room and immediately saw my reflection in the mirror. *What's that dark thing on my lip?* I went closer and realized chocolate was dripping down my lip and chin, creating a black smear. *Oh, no, how long has that been there?*

Remembering when I'd eaten the cookie, I realized it had decorated my face during most of my conversation with the women's ministry director. For whatever reason, she had not felt comfortable telling me about it—and evidently neither had anyone else when we took the photograph! *Oh, Lord, what have You done to me? What about my pithy statements and wise admonitions? How foolish I must have looked being so serious and intense with chocolate running down my chin. How humiliating!*

In a flash of truth, I recognized my pride and arrogance. And I started laughing. Oh, the irony of the contrast of my pride with chocolate trickling down my chin! *Oh, Lord, You do have a sense of humor, don't You?* I continued to chuckle as I wiped the goo off my face. *Well, Father, I stand corrected. Please forgive me for my pride and self-importance. I fell into that trap again!*

If you can't tell, one of my biggest struggles in maintaining an eternal perspective is remaining humble. Certainly, humility is not the same as humiliation, but God does use interesting tactics to help us see ourselves through His eyes. Humility both creates a divine attitude and is the fruit of an eternal point of view. Humility is so important to God that Micah 6:8 tells us: "He has told you, O man, what is good; and what does the LORD require of you but to do justice, to love kindness, and to walk humbly with your God?"

As I prepared to write this chapter, I happened to be talking with my friend Cherie Montgomery. When I asked her to define humility, she said, "A person who acts the way they really are and not the way others want them to be." Another friend, Bonnie Jeffers, gave me this definition of pride: "Pride is being more concerned about what others think of me (or what I think of myself) than focusing on loving other people." I love both Cherie's and Bonnie's insights because a person who is being insincere and is thinking more of herself than others deserves to have soft, melted chocolate dribble down her lip and chin—and to have her picture taken that way! (No wonder they never sent me a copy of the photo!)

The Roots of Pride

Although the world may not come out directly and encourage us to "be proud," that attitude is foundational for many of the attitudes in our society. Pride is often at the root of a person's desire to climb the corporate ladder. It can encourage another to spend more time working than paying attention to his or her family. It creates a desire to buy on credit so that one can brag, "We have everything the Joneses do." It prevents people from bonding together with others for help or fellowship because they don't want to appear to be needy.

Because pride is a focus on self, it can be expressed in many different ways that we might not identify as pride. For instance, one of my friends identified it in her mother who insists on wrapping her husband's Christmas gifts for his business clients and employees along with the ones for her family. Then she tells everyone, with a tone of martyrdom, "I wrapped 156 Christmas gifts this year." Her son commented, "Mother, no one counts how many gifts she wraps except you." That woman was trying to make people focus on her self-sacrifice, and that indicates her pride.

Pride can also be exhibited as fear of other people's criticism. One woman I heard of told her husband she wanted their new car to be the same color as the old one. The reason? "That way, people won't notice we have a new car." As a Christian, this woman thought having something new would somehow reflect badly on Jesus. Some people wrongly define godliness as wearing dowdy clothing or not spending money to get their hair done. Others think they can't spend the wealth God has provided because "people will think we're not very spiritual if they know we have money." All of these attitudes are the fruit of pride: paying more attention to self than focusing on loving others.

In this chapter, we'll be emphasizing additional ingredients and causes of pride: jealousy and envy, competitiveness, defensiveness, and fear of delegating. Although we may not immediately identify their connection to pride and a lack of humility, they indeed cause us to be dishonest about who we really are and to focus more on ourselves than on loving others. God hates all these sources of pride because the proud person exalts herself over Him. Pride creates jealousy, envy, and impatience. Proverbs tell us it brings quarreling (13:10), precedes disaster (16:18), is a precursor of destruction (18:12), is sinful (21:4), and results in humiliation (29:23). But repeatedly Proverbs tell us that humility brings honor with God and others.

Jealousy and Envy

Last year, another Christian writer and fellow speaker sent me a letter and a survey for an article she was writing. The subject? Envy and jealousy within the ranks of Christian writers and speakers. I cringed when I received her letter because I knew how I struggle with jealousy and envy toward other writers and speakers. I had long ago identified that those ugly temptations were the result of my pride. I have even wept over my inability to conquer those green-eyed monsters.

Thomas Fuller said, "Envy shooteth at others and woundeth herself."[1] I knew I was hurting myself through my envy, yet whenever I would hear of a writer given an opportunity to write an article, I would think, "I could have written that. Why didn't they ask me?" If a speaker friend was invited to speak at a major event, I immediately thought, "I want to do that. Why didn't they invite me?" These kinds of thoughts tormented me. No matter how much I grieved my sinful responses, I rarely had an immediate sense of joy over the opportunities and successes of others.

On my friend's survey, I shared my struggle honestly. When she asked each person to rate their battle with envy on a scale of one to ten, with great sadness I wrote ten, indicating its strong hold over me during that particular season of my life. Later, she told me I was the only one who had written ten. Honesty may be admirable, but I was ashamed.

Matthew A. Castille wrote, "Envy is a sickness that only faith can heal."[2] Since I filled out that survey, God has worked within me to more often replace envy with faith; as a result, pride doesn't have as strong a hold over me as before (and I'm very proud of that!). Later in this chapter I'll share the ways God helped me begin to release that stronghold in my life.

Competitiveness

Closely related to jealousy and envy, competitiveness can make us want to appear more successful than others. "One-upmanship" can quickly seize us in pride's grip. How often have we heard parents bragging about how much more accomplished their children are than someone else's? If someone is sharing how she led her relative to Christ, someone else may interject about how she witnessed to some famous person. If a ministry director is attending a conference of other leaders, she may be tempted to tell about the great success of her Christmas event after hearing of the success of someone's retreat. In large and small ways, it's easy to slip into competing with each other in order to come out on top, to appear more successful, effective, loving . . . whatever . . . than someone else.

One woman who shared with me about her struggle with competitiveness said that watching her cousin speak before a group made her question the ways God had been using her in a local women's shelter. Her influence seemed small in comparison to her cousin's impact on large groups. This woman's feelings are evidence of a typical way our enemy schemes to make us compare ourselves to others.

But when we realize we're a part of the body of Christ, we don't have to succumb to such a low sense of value. In Christ's kingdom, we're all on the same level, working toward the same objective: the glorification of Jesus. Joseph Stowell wrote about the perspective we citizens of heaven should have: "When I accepted the invitation to serve Christ at the Moody Bible Institute, a friend said to me, 'You really took a step up!' He obviously had not yet been gripped with a sense of kingdom identity. There are no 'steps up' in the kingdom. There are only servants who are sovereignly assigned to strategic places in the vineyard. This sense of identity unifies us as one in Him."[3] I need to remember that.

Defensiveness

Unfortunately, there's more. In my pride, I defend myself and rationalize my faults. I become protective of my image. I'm often concerned about what others think of me. I don't want fellow Christians or unbelievers to see my imperfections. It hurts my self-image to know someone has seen a chink in my well-polished armor! And if my weaknesses are revealed, I want to justify my actions by explaining the reasons behind my behavior.

One time when a woman confronted me about a way I'd treated her, I defended myself, refusing to believe I'd done anything wrong. In time, God showed me I had mistreated her and I acknowledged it. Because I went through that very painful experience, I'm learning to be willing to admit failure and wrong choices. In the past, I even thought it benefited Christ's image for me to come across as without shortcomings. After all, I reasoned, if people think I'm needy, they'll think Jesus hasn't met my needs and can't meet their needs. But such pride keeps us from sharing ourselves honestly—which actually makes us attractive and real.

Another way defensiveness rears its ugly head was expressed by Carole. She lost her father about ten years ago but didn't grieve in front of anyone because she thought it would show weakness. She still struggles with letting anyone comfort her when she's crying. She says, "I usually cry in the privacy of my home, yet I long for a friend to just hold me and be there while I grieve. I'd never seen this as pride until recently and it's kind of scary how much pride really does overtake our lives without our realizing it. How come I would never judge anyone else as being weak while grieving and yet I judge myself?"

Carole is learning to be more vulnerable with others as she develops an eternal perspective. When we see things through God's eyes, we don't mind appearing weak, because only Jesus is truly strong.

Fear of Delegating

Herbert Lockyer wrote, "It is a greater achievement to set three men to work than to do the work of three men."[4] Unfortunately, pride can prevent us from acting on that truth. When we lack humility, we have a fear of delegating and we can't allow others to take the ball and run with it. If we're counseling someone, we want to control his or her every action, because we consider him or her a reflection of ourselves. Or our fear of delegating can be as small as not allowing a child to help make cookies because we want the cookies to be perfect for serving at our party.

Just recently, I asked to be taped at one of my speaking engagements. The director of Women's Ministries said she would tape my talk and send it to me later. A few days after the event, she wrote and said, "I'm sorry, I can't send you the tape of your speech. I had assigned someone to turn on the tape recorder and thought she had. But when I noticed the sound levels weren't jumping during your talk, I realized it hadn't been turned on correctly. Because the machine was at the front of the room by you, I chose not to go over and fix it because I felt it would embarrass her. I'm sorry."

Of course, I replied that it was no problem. I admired that leader risking my potential frustration in favor of not embarrassing a fellow worker. Her temptation, however, might be not to delegate such a task in the future. Will she protect her own reputation, or will she be willing to risk it for the potential growth in leadership skills of one of her helpers? Many a ministry has died because the founder wouldn't release hold of her "baby." Although the original vision needs to be encouraged and fostered, having a death grip on a ministry's outcome isn't humility. It's fear and distrust of God's ability to fulfill His plan.

Someone has pointed out that if a church is a healthy one, people will have the freedom to make mistakes. As one of my friends says, "If we can't make mistakes in the presence of our church family, then where can we? When a church allows others to find their niche by trial and error with no condemnation for flubbing up, that is what truly pleases God." I agree with her. It's a humble church that isn't afraid of criticism by Christians and unbelievers alike.

A Biblical Perspective of Humility

The Greek word for humility had previously been used by heathen writers to communicate something negative: "groveling" or "abject." But the apostle Paul communicated it as a worthy attitude when seeing life through God's eyes.

True humility is not to think low of oneself but to think rightly and truthfully of oneself. Romans 12:3 gives God's perspective: "For through the grace given to me I say to every man among you not to think more highly of himself than he ought to think; but to think so as to have sound judgment, as God has allotted to each a measure of faith." Author Warren Wiersbe wrote: "It is important that we understand what the Bible means by 'humility.' The humble person is not one who thinks meanly of himself; he simply does not think of himself at all! (I think Andrew Murray said that.) Humility is that grace that, when you know you have it, you have lost it. The truly humble person knows himself and accepts himself (Romans 12:3). He yields himself to Christ to be a servant, to use what he is and has for the glory of God and the good of others."[5]

Having an eternal perspective allows us to credit God—not ourselves—for the work He does in our lives. Humility is not putting ourselves down, but acknowledging the strengths God has given us and the work He has done through us. It can be summed up through a word picture I heard several years ago. Sometimes a turtle can be found balanced on a fence post in the yards of Midwestern towns. No one believes that turtle climbed up there himself.

No, he was placed there. You and I are like that turtle. God places us in ministry or service whether it's called parenting, employment, ministry, volunteering, or listening. We didn't climb onto those opportunities ourselves. If we had, we couldn't expect Him to empower us to do the job He's given us. But we didn't. And because it's all His doing and not our own, we can give Him all the praise and glory.

When you and I are in heaven, the Bible says we will cast our crowns before the throne, saying, "Worthy art Thou, our Lord and our God, to receive glory and honor and power; for Thou didst create all things, and because of Thy will they existed, and were created" (Revelation 4:11). Someday you and I will cast our crowns before God's throne, undeserving of their worth, because God was the source of our abilities, the inspiration for our good deeds, and the Creator of our opportunities.

God is the One who deserves the praise. As we keep that uppermost in our minds, our earthly perspective will be replaced by a divine sense of proportion.

To strengthen our heavenly perspective, Paul offers us the ultimate example of humility in Philippians 2:5-8. And of course, we're not surprised to find that it's none other than Jesus. "Have this attitude in yourself which was also in Christ Jesus, who, although He existed in the form of God, did not regard equality with God a thing to be grasped, but emptied Himself, taking the form of a bond-servant, and being made in the likeness of men. And being found in appearance as a man, He humbled Himself by becoming obedient to the point of death, even death on a cross."

Jesus willingly sacrificed His ability to have His human needs met in supernatural ways. He was hungry and tempted in the wilderness when He could have had angels ministering to Him night and day. He grew tired walking when He could have called for a heavenly chariot to transport Him. He felt the sting of rejection when He could have called fire from heaven to consume His enemies. He humbled Himself, taking on our human nature for one grand purpose: to reveal the Father's love through sacrificing His own life on a cross. He reveals for us that humility is the surrendering of having things done the way we think they should be done and, instead, cooperating with the Father's plan.

Cultivating Humility

As my desire to see myself and the world through God's eyes has grown, I've learned that I need to take an active part in diminishing my pride. First, I must consciously welcome humility by surrendering to God's supernatural work in my heart. With so much fuel for our pride, it may seem almost impossible to achieve humility. And it *is* impossible when we see it as an "achievement" or as the goal. But when we realize that humility is something that forms within us while we're focused on Christ, we can learn to depend on God to develop it in us as we surrender ourselves to Him.

Second, I must learn to follow Paul's example by boasting legitimately about God's work in me. Third, I must practice taking captive my prideful thoughts and replacing them with God's perspective. Fourth, I must let God choose the specific ways in which He uses me to fulfill His plans. And finally, I must bless those whom God chooses to use and honor.

Depend on God

In practical terms, humility can be summed up in the words of author Thomas á Kempis: "Strive to do another's will rather than your own. Choose always to have less than more. Seek the lower places in life, dying to the need to be recognized and important. Always and in everything, desire that the will of God may be completely fulfilled in you." I've determined that Thomas á Kempis's words are my life's Purpose Statement. I have them posted on the wall in front of my desk. They are a constant reminder to allow God to form humility within me as I focus on Jesus' example.

If I wake up in the morning and pray, "Lord, I want to be humble today," I begin to focus on putting others first. That's good. The day proceeds and a friend drops by to visit unexpectedly. Even though I'm thinking of my long "to-do" list, the Lord seems to say, "She's hurting. Spend some time with her." I remember my morning prayer to be humble and that means "striving to do another's will rather than your own" as Thomas á Kempis encourages me. So, I patiently listen to my friend.

As I do, I smugly think, "All right, Lord, I achieved my humility of mind today. Thanks for answering my prayer." My chest puffs out and I mentally pat myself on the back. I am progressing, aren't I? Suddenly, I realize that pride has just promptly kicked out my humility and I'm back to focusing on myself. Drat! I thought I'd made some progress! How can I ever be humble if I'm so aware of what I've accomplished?

Author Richard Foster wrote, "Suppose I am longing to win the battle over pride. (I know that today people are not much concerned about pride, but the devotional masters always saw it as among the most destructive sins.) I can never defeat pride by 'trying.' Direct assault against pride will only make me proud of my humility!"[6]

Sheila shared with me the solution for the dilemma expressed by Richard Foster. One day as she was rehearsing with her church's worship team, she asked the Lord to keep them humble as they were up in front of the congregation. God said to her, "The only thing you can do is to ask for Jesus' mantle of humility. If you work up your own humility then you will be proud because you did it."

That's the first key to cultivating humility: Consciously choose to depend on God by "getting out of the way" and making room for Jesus to form His character within you.

Boast Legitimately

The second key is based in the fact that the apostle Paul doesn't seem to have difficulty speaking of God's wonderful work within him. He calls it "boasting" and he writes about it many times in Scripture. For instance:

> Therefore in Christ Jesus I have found reason for boasting in things pertaining to God. For I will not presume to speak of anything except what Christ has accomplished through me, resulting in the obedience of the Gentiles by word and deed, in the power of signs and wonders, in the power of the Spirit; so that from Jerusalem and round about as far as Illyricum I have fully preached the gospel of Christ. (Romans 15:17-19)

> But let each one examine his own work, and then he will have reason for boasting in regard to himself alone, and not in regard to another. (Galatians 6:4)

> But may it never be that I should boast, except in the cross of our Lord Jesus Christ, through which the world has been crucified to me, and I to the world. (Galatians 6:14)

> For I am the least of the apostles, who am not fit to be called an apostle, because I persecuted the church of God. But by the grace of God I am what I am, and His grace toward me did not prove vain; but I labored even more than all of them, yet not I, but the grace of God with me. (1 Corinthians 15:9-10)

> But we will not boast beyond our measure, but within the measure of the sphere which God apportioned to us as a measure, to reach even as far as you. . . . But He who boasts, let him boast in the Lord. For not he who commends himself is approved, but whom the Lord commends. (2 Corinthians 10:13,17-18)

Paul doesn't hesitate to boast about what God has done through him! Author Gene Getz calls Paul's balanced eternal perspective about humility "legitimate pride." He explains that this is based not on "his human accomplishments, but in the fact that others are in heaven and that he would be able to present them to Christ in an act of worship and love."[7]

What can we learn from Paul's "legitimate pride" as we seek an eternal perspective about humility?

- It's Okay to boast, as long as the boasting is based in Jesus' work through us.
- Giving God glory in His working through us is not pride; it's true humility.
- Boasting should be only about God's work.
- We shouldn't base our humility in comparing ourselves to others. The basis for humility is not whether we've done better or more poorly than another.
- Humility can get excited about what God is doing! We can say, "I have really grown in my ability to do . . . or be . . . or demonstrate . . ." As long as we're giving the glory to God, that's "legitimate boasting."
- Our knowledge of God's work must be based in His grace. Grace means that I don't deserve to be used by God to accomplish His purposes. Grace means that out of God's mercy and generosity, He chooses to use each one of us—and He doesn't even need us! He could complete all His plans without any of our help, yet He chooses to use our inadequate efforts and inefficient methods. Any results are totally due to His work within our hearts and lives.

My sister Karen shared an incident with me that expresses how God wants us to boast of His grace. She was attending a Christian conference and was fuming inside because she had been standing in line at the bookstore for at least twenty minutes and the line was not moving at all. She focused in on the operations at the sales desk and noticed that there were at least five people working with customers but the line never moved. She says, "I couldn't imagine what could be taking so long. I was anxious to hear the current speaker at the conference so I felt angry. If I ran my restaurant like this, I wouldn't stay in business. I always try to anticipate problems at the restaurant so my customers aren't inconvenienced, but it was obvious these people hadn't planned well."

Karen didn't recognize right away that pride had entered her thinking. But as she stood there fuming, the Holy Spirit began to nudge her about her attitude. Karen began to argue with Him, reminding Him that she had come one hundred miles to the conference and was missing it while these people were ineffective and disorganized. Karen says, "The Lord began to impress upon me that I needed to ask Him for grace for the situation and to recognize my pride. My first reaction was that the bookstore had the problem, not me. If they would only get their act together then I wouldn't have to ask for grace. But gently the Holy Spirit continued to speak to my heart and I began to pray for the grace that God desired to give me. Almost immediately the line began to move, however slowly."

By the time Karen got to the counter, she had prayed for grace for herself for a good ten minutes and began to feel her heart soften. The woman who finally waited on her expressed her extreme frustration because of a problem with their credit card machine. Because Karen dealt with credit cards at her restaurant, she was able to identify the problem and help solve it. Karen says, "I was extremely thankful for the time I had been praying for grace to overcome my pride so that when I arrived at the counter I didn't yell at the frazzled volunteer. I was able to calmly pay my bill and leave the bookstore."

When Karen returned to her seat beside her friend, Melanie, she was able to share with her about how God had worked in her attitude. That's "legitimate boasting!"

If we don't have a correct sense of humility, we might feel like we shouldn't acknowledge the ways God works in and through us. Many years ago, I heard a speaker whose words touched me. I expressed my appreciation to her and she replied, "I'm so glad God spoke to you." Somehow I felt as if she weren't acknowledging my point: that God had used *her* to do this. I wanted her to know that because I wanted to bless her!

When I reworded my gratitude, she again gave a response that didn't seem to acknowledge her involvement. I walked away frustrated, even angry. Why couldn't she receive my thanks? Although her response may have seemed a humble one, I actually felt she appeared proud.

Maybe I overreacted, but a simple "thank you" to acknowledge when someone is expressing his or her gratitude to us is appropriate when we recognize that God is using us to showcase His glory. We can also add, "Isn't the Lord good?" or "I'm so glad God blessed you" as a way of directing attention to God's work. I believe that's how Paul would have responded to those who might thank him. He wouldn't say, "Oh, it was nothing I did. God did it all!" No, Paul boasted of God's work through him. That's not pride. That's humility.

In Mary, the mother of Jesus, we see another example of the kind of humility God desires. When the angel Gabriel appeared to Mary to announce that she would bear the Messiah, this *isn't* what happened:

Mary looked at the angel in surprise. "Me?" she cried out. "Oh, no, I'm sure God has it all wrong. I'm just an insignificant nobody that God can't use. Surely you must have turned down the wrong street. You most likely meant to go to Martha's house on the next block. Now there's a gal who deserves to be used by God. I sure don't."

If Mary had responded in that way, she would have been exemplifying pride—an arrogance that doesn't acknowledge or surrender to God's ability to use a person. Instead, after an initial shock, Mary accepts God's will by humbly saying, "Behold, the bondslave of the

Lord; be it done to me according to your word" (Luke 1:38). Then Mary travels to Elizabeth's house and rejoices at her cousin's greeting: "Blessed among women are you, and blessed is the fruit of your womb!" (Luke 1:42). Again, Mary doesn't reject Elizabeth's exclamation of the truth. She receives it and exalts God in song, giving Him the glory and lifting Him up. Even as she does that she acknowledges her own "humble state of His bondslave; For behold, from this time on all generations will count me blessed. For the Mighty One has done great things for me; And holy is His name" (Luke 1:48-49).

Humility doesn't discredit God's work through us; it acknowledges God's enabling and then directs the listener to God. Conference speaker Tony Evans sums it up by saying, "God never meant for His blessings on your life and mine to produce pride. The more we are blessed, the more humble we should be. The more we have, the lower we should go.

"But we have this thing turned the wrong way in the upside-down kingdom of earth. The more we have, the higher our shoulders go, the higher our heads are raised. That's why of the seven sins God hates, pride tops the list (Proverbs 6:16-17) because pride says, 'I pulled myself up by my own bootstraps.' What God says is, 'I gave you the boots! I put them on you.' So we are to think about our blessings with the mind of Christ, which tells us we are blessed that we might make a difference among men for the glory of God."[8]

Take Every Proud Thought Captive

As we seek to replace pride with legitimate boasting, we can apply the principle found in 2 Corinthians 10:5: "We are taking every thought captive to the obedience of Christ." The truth of that Scripture is one of the tools God is using to help me resist pride.

I understand that I don't actually "own" a thought until I agree with it. Jesus had sinful thoughts while being tempted, but because He rejected those thoughts with the truth, He did not sin.

Our own thoughts are like arrows within our minds. These thoughts are "aimed" at us from three possible sources: God, ourselves, or Satan. When we become aware of them, we have a choice either to let them penetrate us and become part of us or protect ourselves from them.

Of course, every thought from God needs to be welcomed and agreed with, but those from ourselves or Satan could be suspect. Therefore, we need to grab each "arrow" and examine it with the question, "Is this really the way I want to think? Is this the way God wants me to think?" At that point, the idea is not part of us, it just has the potential to be ours. If it's not the way God wants us to think, we can cast it away before we agree with it. In that way we conquer sin.

In my own life, when a jealous arrow labeled, "Oh, why didn't they ask me to do that? I would do a better job" takes aim, I can take it captive and refuse to agree with it. I can consciously counter it by thinking, "God has chosen that person and not me. He knows who will fulfill His plan best. I don't need to be jealous. God will choose me for the things He wants me to do." Although my feelings might not immediately agree with my chosen thoughts, that doesn't matter. God doesn't judge me by my feelings, but by what I choose to believe.

I can also apply that principle to a competitive arrow labeled, "Well, if she can talk about her son making the honor roll, I can brag about my daughter being captain of the drill team." By quickly rejecting it with, "No, I'm going to rejoice with my friend. I might share about my daughter's success, but not in order to compete." At that point, I've maintained my humility.

Further, a "fear of delegating" arrow might appear with writing on it that says, "I'd better not ask Linda to work on that project because she might not do as good a job as me, and the boss is watching." I can ask God's power to choose a different response: "Lord, if you want Linda to learn from this project, then I can risk my own reputation. I'll walk her through it."

Such relaxing in God's power strengthens our humility muscle. In all these circumstances, we are actively involved in rejecting ungodly thoughts and making right choices, but it's God who actually forms the humility within us.

Let God Choose

As I applied the concept of taking every thought captive to the obedience of Christ, God showed me another way to diminish my pride, especially regarding competitive thinking. I began meditating on the fact that God indeed chooses which of His children will best fulfill His plan. I could focus either on what He hadn't chosen me for, or on what He had. And I realized He had chosen me for many opportunities! In His graciousness, He had chosen me. Me! I knew that was totally His grace because only in His power could I do anything. Gratitude replaced my competitive and proud spirit. I realized I wasn't neglected after all. I rejoiced in knowing God valued my service, even if He didn't give me every opportunity I thought I should have.

Have you been feeling upset because the choir director chose someone else to sing the solo for the Easter cantata and you thought you would do it? Be grateful for the past opportunities the director has given you. Have you been angry because your boss delegated an important training opportunity to a fellow worker and you thought you could do a better job? Be grateful that such an assignment won't take additional time away from your family. Have you been disgruntled because God hasn't given you the blessing of having children? Look for the opportunity of ministering to the needs of the children of a single parent and see how God blesses you in that.

Janice identified her pride after her daughter wasn't chosen for the high school basketball varsity squad. It was obvious to her how her daughter was more talented than the others the coach had chosen, and Janice was angry. But then the Lord showed her that her anger was masking her pride. He seemed to indicate, "You want this for Cindy but she's not ready for it. I'm protecting her from something that will be destructive. Your pride is blinding you to what's best for her." Janice accepted God's correction and acknowledged that she needed to allow God to choose what was best for her daughter.

I will never forget the time God impressed upon me how crucial it is to allow Him to decide what's best for each of His children and which ones He uses to represent Him at different times. I had heard about another woman's invitation to speak before a large group. This woman had experienced great trials and terrible grief. Out of her brokenness God raised up a tremendous ministry. But I believed I could do as good a job as she could.

I quickly recognized my old enemy and, as I prayed about my rising sense of pride (in the form of envy), the Lord seemed to whisper in my heart, "Do you want to experience all the trials and grief that she has? You are envious of so many; do you want to go through all that they have so that you can have their writing and speaking ministries?"

Like Job in Job 40:4-5, I clapped my hand over my mouth in awe. "Lord, I've never looked at it that way. You do use people because of what they've learned through their trials and sorrows. I would have to experience all they've gone through to have the same opportunities. Oh, Lord, no! I repent in dust and ashes, and close my mouth on my proud thoughts."

That revelation seemed to put a large chain on the door blocking pride's entrance into my heart. Oh, at times jealousy, envy, and competitive responses still try to break that chain and move in. But the door doesn't swing open quite as wide. I'm learning to relax in the fact that whoever gets the credit, the opportunities, or the invitations is fine, as long as Jesus is lifted up. That's having an eternal perspective.

Bless Others

When Janice repented of her prideful desires regarding her daughter's participation on the basketball team, she discovered another key for reversing pride, especially for that humility-stealer, envy.

"I made a conscious choice to bless the coach and the other players who made the team instead of Cindy," she said.

I practice this principle regularly. When I hear of someone's opportunity and the old envy rises within my heart, I quickly pray, "Lord, bless that person in this endeavor. Use her mightily to draw others to You. Give her abundant success, for she serves You with an eager heart." Acknowledging that God is the One in charge tamps down my rising pride and helps me to praise God for His blessings in others' lives as well as my own.

My friend Susan practiced this principle when she began to envy her sister-in-law's large new home. Susan says, "As soon as I realized what I was doing, I started praying and asking God to bless them more and continue to do so. My envious feelings started to evaporate."

Author Richard B. Douglass wrote, "The modern American seldom pauses to give thanks for the simple blessings of life. One reason is that we are used to having so much. We simply assume that we will have all the good things of life. Another reason is that it hurts our pride to be grateful. We do not want to admit that God is the Provider of all good things. We are simply His stewards. Being thankful requires humility and faith in God. When we have these, we can be grateful."[9]

The Rewards of Humility

As we allow God to make changes in our thinking and responding so that a heavenly perspective of humility permeates our being, God promises that we will be honored. First Peter 5:6 assures us, "Humble yourselves, therefore, under the mighty hand of God, that He may exalt you at the proper time." Jesus promises in Matthew 23:12: "And whoever exalts himself shall be humbled; and whoever humbles himself shall be exalted." Although being exalted shouldn't be our motivation for righteous living, it certainly can encourage us to allow God to form humility in our hearts.

But if the reward is delayed, it's easy to become discouraged. The story is told of Henry Morrison, who after serving in Africa for forty years as a missionary, returned to America aboard a ship that also carried Theodore Roosevelt. As the passengers disembarked, there was great fanfare for the President. Henry grew discouraged wondering why his humble service wasn't acknowledged in some way. But then within Henry's heart, the Lord whispered, "Don't worry, Henry. You're not home yet!"

Though we may not receive the rewards of our humility on earth, God tells us, "Don't worry, my child. The reception you'll receive in your heavenly home will far outweigh whatever you might receive on earth. In fact, don't desire adoration on earth, for it will dilute what you receive in heaven. My thanks and praise of 'well done, thou good and faithful servant' will be more valuable than any accolades you receive on earth."

That doesn't mean God won't ever allow us to receive praise from our fellow heavenly citizens. He often does. But we won't receive all of the honor God has in store for us until we are in His presence. And with God, nothing done in His power will be exempt from His gratitude.

In our next chapter, we'll examine the eternal perspective of being able to forgive, even when bitterness haunts us. Have you been deeply wounded by someone? Don't let the pain of the past steal your hope for the future.

⇥ *Questions* ⇤

1. Have you ever had an experience similar to the one I shared about the chocolate on my lip and chin? Were you angry and humiliated, or could you laugh?

2. If you are dissatisfied with your response, what would you like your attitude to be the next time in a similar situation?

3. What number on a scale of one to ten would you have assigned yourself for my friend's survey (page 119)?

4. What contributes to your jealousy or envy? What helps to minimize it?

5. Of the four different ingredients of pride I discussed (jealousy and envy, competition, defensiveness, and fear of delegating) which do you struggle with most?

6. Memorize Romans 12:3. Is there some situation you anticipate in the future when that verse could help you maintain
   greater humility? If so, how will you apply it?

7. According to Revelation 4:11, why should God receive glory?
   How can the truth of that verse help you keep a humble
   attitude?

8. Review the verses on pages 127-128. Indicate what inspires
   you from each.

   Romans 15:17-19:

   Galatians 6:4:

   Galatians 6:14:

   1 Corinthians 15:9-10:

   2 Corinthians 10:13,17-18:

9. What qualities and opportunities has God given you that you
   can "boast legitimately" about?

10. Read Jesus' mother's account in Luke 1:26-56. What principles about a godly response to God's blessing can you draw from Mary's example?

11. Consider the five principles for diminishing pride discussed in this chapter:

- Depend on God
- Boast legitimately
- Take every proud thought captive
- Let God choose
- Bless others

Which is most helpful to you? Why?

12. In what ways have your attitudes or perceptions about humility been altered by reading this chapter? How will these new attitudes affect your daily life?

Forgiveness

I can forgive past hurt and look forward to the future.

Remember St. Teresa's bold saying that from heaven the most miserable earthly life will look like one bad night in an inconvenient hotel!

PETER KRAFT

What matters isn't what happens to you but what happens in you.

UNKNOWN

I MET PEGGY MCDERMOTT AT A WOMEN'S RETREAT AND SHE TOLD me her story: For many years, Peggy blamed God for the abuse that came in all forms in her childhood. "I couldn't understand how God could stand by and allow those things to happen to me. I did know there was a God but I didn't have any sense that He was real, and if He was, I certainly wasn't worthy of His time or thought."

Eventually, she followed her daughter Jessica to church and the women there helped her to see that God did indeed love her. She accepted Christ as her Savior. As she began to work through the great wounds inflicted in her childhood, she realized, "God never promised that my life would be easy. I needed to give Him all the broken pieces of my life because He couldn't do His work with only a few. I'm learning not to take these pieces back until the Lord is finished with them, for it is only then that God shows Himself to me."

But letting God do His healing work hasn't always been easy for Peggy. At times, her memories were overwhelming. She struggled with a recurrent picture of abuse that was particularly vivid, even to the point that she had to stop her car on the road to avoid vomiting when this picture invaded her mind. At those times, she couldn't understand how the Lord could love her and still watch that happen to a little child.

But then in October 1993, at her church's women's retreat, through the speaker and the love of her sisters in Christ, the Lord assured Peggy that when all those traumas occurred, He was not only with her but He cried too. He was not a bystander. And now He would take all the broken pieces of her soul and create a beautiful whole that would glorify Him.

For the first time Peggy knew she was not alone and that her whole life was in God's hands. "The memories of what I went through will never go completely away," she says. "They are a part of me. But the continued pain and suffering that was haunting me through visions, nightmares, and feelings of helplessness and hopelessness are now gone. I realize that my behavior as a result of being a victim was less than desirable, and it's only *my* behavior that the Lord will hold me accountable for."

Peggy has learned the invaluable lesson that when we are willing to let go of the past, God will heal our wounds and even use our past suffering for good in the future.

Beyond Bitterness

No one makes it through this life without being hurt and hurting others. Many women have shared with me their pain from being abused as children. Others have experienced the trauma of losing beloved family members in car accidents because of a drunk driver. Many women are angry at their husbands for their infidelity. Others are angry at God because some of their dreams have gone unfulfilled. Still other women are bitter toward themselves because of mistakes they've made. The possibilities are endless.

Our earthly perspective makes it seem right to remain bitter about past offenses. Our natural reaction is to enjoy our pain! That seems strange, yet it's true. I've experienced it myself. Initially, my resentment feels good. It allows me to focus on myself, and my hatred and self-pity seem justified. But in time, that resentment grows into bitterness and, like a poisonous root, it begins to infect my thinking and my responses. It bears the fruit of anger, discontentment, self-absorption, paranoia, and despair.

Christian psychologists Kevin Downing and Peter Robbins have summarized the results of bitterness in a little booklet called "Beyond Bitterness." They list these negative consequences:

- Bitterness blinds us to the things we have the power to change and influence.
- Bitterness consumes our lives. It may take the form of

obsession as we constantly rehearse the hurts we've
encountered.

- Bitterness isolates us from others and God. It can begin to
make everyone else an enemy.
- Bitterness makes us into the very thing we hate and want
to avoid.
- Bitterness destroys our physical bodies.[1]

The longer we allow the fruit of bitterness to rot within us, the
greater its disastrous effect. We think we're hurting the person who
harmed us, but usually he or she is blissfully unaware of our pain.
Sometimes, that person does try to reconcile with us, but the anger
and resentment we have nursed over months or years prevents us
from forgiving. In those moments, we are like the foolish person
described in Proverbs 18:19: "An offended brother is more unyielding than a fortified city, and disputes are like the barred gates of a
citadel." Bitterness creates a wall of protection that we might think
helps us, but in reality it locks us within a fortress of hate and self-
destruction.

Don't get me wrong: Forgiveness is not intended to swing open
the door to further destructive behavior from others. Forgiveness
sets us free from bitterness, but it's not designed to free others to
continue making our lives miserable. Rather, forgiving means letting go of anger and the need to punish someone. Forgiveness often
requires a difficult decision to relinquish the desire for revenge. If
we have been hurt over a long period of time or the pain was deep,
the process of forgiveness can take a long time.

Stephanie had to learn a lot about biblical forgiveness after years
of hating her parents. Her father was an alcoholic and her mother
beat her often. When she became a Christian twenty years ago, God
immediately began dealing with the anger and bitterness stored up
in her heart toward her parents. After years of counseling, she was
willing to forgive the hurts of the past but she still felt paralyzed in
dealing with her parents in the present. They remained difficult,

unhappy people who never asked for her forgiveness or acknowledged the hurt they'd caused her. In fact, Stephanie's mother
frequently referred to what a great mother she'd been.

Stephanie says, "After forgiving them, the next step was being
willing to be reconciled with them. This was a huge struggle for
me because in my mind the only way I could be reconciled with
them was to be abused by them again. I thought it meant being
totally at their mercy. This was a lie, and God very graciously sent
a woman to pray with me about this at a conference I was attending.
As a result, God helped me say 'no' to their abuse. He helped me
see their manipulation and how to respond to it. He was my pro-
tector and He helped me set boundaries. That same year my father
died. We did not have a perfect kind of reconciliation, but I am at
peace. I do not hate my parents and I have forgiven them."

I admire Stephanie for her willingness to journey toward forgiveness. Each of us can make that same choice with God's help.
If we want to have an eternal perspective, we must put aside our
bitterness and seek godly wisdom. How can we do that? Paul gives
us the key in Philippians 3:13-14. He writes, "Brethren, I do not
regard myself as having laid hold of it yet; but one thing I do: forgetting what lies behind and reaching forward to what lies ahead,
I press on toward the goal for the prize of the upward call of God
in Christ Jesus." When we are tempted to focus on the past and be
bitter, we can follow Paul's example to develop a heavenly frame
of mind.

Don't Fret the Past

The first thing we can do to see the hurtful things that happen in
our lives through God's eyes is to stop dwelling on the past. This
doesn't mean "don't remember" the past. In 2 Corinthians 11:23-28,
Paul catalogues a long list of things he suffered: beatings, stonings,
shipwrecks, hunger, danger, and stress from his concern for his spiritual flock. He is "rehearsing" his past, but only as a means of

establishing his point. He doesn't keep his focus there. He doesn't continue to dwell upon his pain. He's not using others' sins as fuel for any resentment. His list of hurts gives him a frame of reference from which to glorify God, but it doesn't "captivate" him—and that's why he's not bitter about it. Like Peggy McDermott, Paul knows that what he experienced will always be a part of him, but it doesn't have to rule him. He sees the purpose in what happened to him and considers it insignificant in comparison to giving glory to God.

Author Warren Wiersbe gives us a valuable insight when he says, "Please keep in mind that in Bible terminology, 'to forget' does not mean 'to fail to remember.' Apart from senility, hypnosis, or a brain malfunction, no mature person can forget what has happened in the past. We may wish that we could erase certain bad memories, but we cannot. 'To forget' in the Bible means 'no longer to be influenced by or affected by.'"[2] In other words, we can remember the past without allowing it to hold us hostage.

Wiersbe continues by clarifying that forgetting the past "simply means that we break the power of the past by living for the future. We cannot change the past, but we can change the meaning of the past. There were things in Paul's past that could have been weights to hold him back (1 Timothy 1:12-17), but they became inspirations to speed him ahead. The events did not change, but his understanding of them changed."[3]

Many of us aspire to forget the hurtful things of the past. We think that will set us free. But that isn't what Paul encourages us to do. In fact, there is value in remembering the past, even if it's painful. If we remember our own past mistakes yet allow God's forgiveness to take away the sting, we'll be less tempted to allow pride to influence us today. Being forgiven nurtures humility. Such humility will also help us respond in a godly fashion to being hurt by others.

Remembering our own past need for forgiveness also leads to compassion for others. Whenever I start to be critical of a young mom trying to control her misbehaving children in the grocery store, the Holy Spirit taps my shoulder gently and says, "Look who's talking. Remember where you came from." That gentle reminder allows me to reflect on the difficulties of being a young mom, rather than thinking every mother should react perfectly. Compassion replaces my critical spirit. If it were possible for me to forget my past sin, I wouldn't be able to have that compassion.

Finally, remembering past hurt, whether caused by self or others, will equip us to help and comfort others who have been similarly hurt. Author Barbara Johnson writes, "Whatever the stress you're facing right now, you WILL get through it. You will win, and after you're a winner, you can reach back and help along another suffering, stressed-out person who needs to hear the good news that she can be a winner, too!"[4] Second Corinthians 1:3-4 tells us the same thing: "Blessed be the God and Father of our Lord Jesus Christ, the father of mercies and God of all comfort; who comforts us in all our affliction so that we may be able to comfort those who are in any affliction with the comfort with which we ourselves are comforted by God." What we learn and remember from our past can be used to strengthen and uplift fellow strugglers.

That's how God used Peggy McDermott. She established a support group at her church named R.O.S.E.S.: Reaching Our Sisters Emotional Strengths. She says, "My vision was to have a safe, loving atmosphere where women can share their concerns without fear of criticism or judgment. They need to be able to confidentially share their story no matter how painful or shocking. My goal is that women can grow and discover that no problem is too small, too big, or too shocking when we have the Lord at our side." Peggy would never have shared that significant help with others if she hadn't experienced what she did.

As you and I testify to God's power and deliverance regarding the healing of our past wounds, or how He pulled us out of bitterness, or how He gives us joy though we've been misunderstood, He will receive the glory. If we could somehow forget what happened,

He could not be given the praise for His work in our lives.

So remember the past, but allow God's grace to remove the sting. Don't misunderstand: Not fretting the past doesn't mean we don't allow ourselves to feel pain. We should deal with our emotions in a real and honest way. Whether we are grieving over a loss or dealing with anger toward someone who gossiped about us, burying those emotions will only cause them to resurface another time in an inappropriate way.

Author Doug Manning writes, "Grieving is as natural as crying when you are hurt, sleeping when you're tired, eating when you're hungry, or sneezing when your nose itches. It's nature's way of healing a broken heart. Don't let anyone take your grief away from you. You deserve it, and you must have it. If you had broken a leg, no one would criticize you for using crutches until it was healed. If you had major surgery, no one would pressure you to run in a marathon the next week. Grief is a major wound. It does not heal overnight. You must have the time and the crutches until you heal."[5]

Marilyn Willett Heavilin, author of *I'm Listening, Lord*, is well acquainted with grief because of the deaths of three sons: one to crib death, one shortly after birth, and one killed as a teen by a drunk driver. A short time after her teenager's death, she was driving to a friend's home and got lost. She suddenly realized she was on the street of the man who had killed her boy. Before she could turn around and escape, she saw him playing ball with his son. She says, "After I turned the corner, I parked the car and cried. I hated it that he—the man who killed my son—could enjoy a summer afternoon with his son. He robbed me of a privilege he was still experiencing. Oh, how I wished he could feel my devastation and my sorrow."

Several months later, when Marilyn saw that same man in the courtroom during the trial, she was able to forgive him because she saw him as the broken man he was. She says, "As I entered the second floor hallway the first day we were to appear in court, I saw the man who killed Nate. He looked like a very frightened man— not a killer at all. I didn't feel angry, nor did I want to scream or lash out at him—I just stood and let the tears fall. God had removed the bitterness and was allowing me to forgive this man."

Marilyn says that forgiveness took time as she allowed herself to experience her emotions. She cautions, "When we are grieving, we shouldn't feel compelled to rush forgiveness. It may be necessary to allow time for the situation to sink in and for God to do a work in our hearts."[6]

Giving ourselves permission to feel our feelings is an important part of the healing process. As we are honest before the Lord and surrender all our feelings to Him, we'll be strengthened to resist bitterness. By turning our attention to Him as quickly as possible, we'll move past the hurt and be able to take the next step in Paul's exhortation in Philippians: Reach for the future.

Reach for the Future

Author Charles Swindoll writes, "Some of the unhappiest people I have ever known are living their lives looking over their shoulder. What a waste! Nothing back there can be changed."[7] How true. When Paul writes, "reaching forward to what lies ahead," he is modeling for us how to stop letting the past grip us and keep us from moving forward.

Paul is using a visual word picture of a common occurrence of his time, the Greek races. Commentators aren't fully agreed about the sport Paul refers to, but Warren Wiersbe prefers the chariot races. He writes, "The Greek chariot, used in the Olympic Games and other events, was really only a small platform with a wheel on each side. The driver had very little to hold on to as he raced around the course. He had to lean forward and strain every nerve and muscle to maintain balance and control the horses."[8] Other theologians prefer the idea of foot races. Ancient Greek stadiums were built with courses for foot races and tiers of seats for spectators. The length of the course in Athens was one-eighth of an old Roman mile, which is 607 feet. The course at Ephesus was slightly longer. The racers were to reach the goal opposite the entrance, or run back and forth—sometimes even twice. Author William Hendricksen explains that "the verb used in the original is very graphic. It pictures the runner straining every nerve and muscle as he keeps on running with all his might toward the goal, his hand stretched out as if to grasp it."[9]

As Christians, Paul wants us to have a joyful anticipation of God's future work through us. As we shake off the shackles of the pain of the past and believe God is empowering us to serve Him, we will have hope about the future.

Hope is essential in our fight against bitterness. Envisioning a powerful outcome from the pain that could create bitterness helps to release its hold over us. As I talk with women and hear the difficult things they've gone through, I frequently encourage them to imagine how God can use it to help others in the future. Usually, they can't imagine it at the time, but often they perk up and say, by faith, "Really? You really think that could happen?" Such a glimpse into how God might use their great suffering or grief begins to set them free from the shackles of bitterness.

While Marilyn Heavilin was in the throes of her grief and anger, she never could have imagined how God would use her in the future to help others travel toward forgiveness. Although she wouldn't have chosen this route, she thanks God for the ways in which He uses her brokenness and redeems her devastation.

If you are struggling with bitterness about a painful circumstance, know that your pain is not in vain. As you imagine how God could use what you are learning, your hope for the future will help you to press on.

Press On in Christ

During the healing process it can be difficult to repeatedly make the choice to stop focusing on the past and instead "press on" in forgiveness. But God commands us to do it, and it's the right thing to do.

I recently heard an example of how doing the right thing can be rewarding, even if it doesn't initially feel like it. In November 1961, a chimpanzee named Enos was hurtling through space in the Atlas rocket. He had been trained to follow ground control's directions because of sixteen weeks of rewards and electric shock punishment. But while in space, the equipment malfunctioned and Enos was shocked when pushing the correct button.

The staff at ground control believed the billion-dollar program would be destroyed—and Enos along with it. But miraculously, Enos continued to push the correct button repeatedly, over and over again. Even though he was shocked every time, he did the right thing! The staff was relieved and surprised. Because of Enos's willingness to endure pain for doing the right thing, the rocket returned to earth and the chimp's life wasn't snuffed out in space. Enos's bravery prepared the way for John Glenn to orbit Earth.

Doing the right thing by forgiving often hurts. Sometimes it shocks us—especially if it doesn't mend the relationship or take away our pain. But it's part of Christ's "upward calling" on our lives. And He not only commands it, He rewards it by giving us peace.

Pattie knows that truth. For many years she was controlled by her anger toward Jim, her brother-in-law, for bringing conflict into their family. When her sister Pam married Jim, her high school sweetheart, he seemed to fit right into their Christian family. But years later, a religious cult swayed Jim's commitment away from Jesus, even though Pam maintained her faith in Christ. Jim wouldn't allow Pam and their sons to see Pattie and her family. Pattie fretted constantly about what they should do. Should they kidnap Pam? Should they try an intervention? She felt frustrated and helpless, and that fueled her anger and bitterness toward Jim. Although she prayed for his return to Jesus, she really wanted to see him pay for the grief he'd brought their family.

After twenty years of praying for Jim's salvation, Pattie saw God do a miracle. Along with Jim, a whole group of Jim's friends in the cult changed their views and believed again the truth about Jesus' gift of salvation. Pattie's family was astounded at God's answer to their prayers and Pattie anticipated that Jim would ask for the family's forgiveness for his hurtful choices.

But it never came. Although he confessed to them his new faith in Christ, he didn't acknowledge the pain he'd caused. Pattie couldn't believe it! She wanted him to say he was sorry! As the families had more contact now, his seeming insensitivity to their past wounds made her even angrier. She wanted the satisfaction of knowing that Jim understood the pain he'd caused and was willing to ask for their forgiveness. However, Pattie says, "In time, I had to recognize that it must have been so difficult for Jim to turn back to the Lord and forsake his old way of thinking that I should be grateful for that huge step. Did I want him not to come back to the Lord because he didn't want to ask our forgiveness? Obviously not. His salvation is too important. Little by little, God is helping me to forgive Jim. My bitterness still surfaces at times but I'm learning to choose to be grateful for the big step he took. God reminds me that that is more important than my getting the satisfaction of hearing Jim's request for our forgiveness."

Sometimes it's not other people who need forgiving: it's ourselves. I recently encountered a woman at a retreat who was having a hard time forgiving herself. I had shared at the Friday evening session how God delivered me from being a child abuser. During the Saturday afternoon free time, I enjoyed visiting privately with many of the women. One woman, Carrie, came into my room looking sheepish. After this attractive thirty-something woman sat down and I asked what was on her heart, she hesitantly began.

"When I heard you share about being a child abuser, I knew you were the one I could talk to." She looked down and her face turned pale. I waited. "You see, I've done something as bad as that and I haven't been able to tell anyone. But when I heard you, I figured you were the one." She glanced up at me quickly and then again averted her eyes.

Taking a deep breath, she whispered, "I had an affair with my husband's best friend. . . ." After pausing, she rushed on, "My husband has forgiven me but I can't seem to forgive myself. I keep asking God to forgive me. I tell Him over and over again, 'I'm sorry . . .' but I never feel forgiven."

I expressed my appreciation for Carrie's willingness to be vulnerable and we talked for a few minutes about forgiveness being a decision, not a feeling. Soon, it was as if a burden had been removed from her shoulders. She could look me straight in the eye and she sat up taller. Confessing her sin to someone else seemed to relieve her of her pain. We prayed together and I took her through a process of asking God to forgive her and help her to forgive herself. I sensed God was working an incredible healing in her heart.

When the next woman knocked at my door to indicate Carrie's time had concluded, Carrie gave me a quick hug, snatched up her Bible and cup of tea, and hurried out the door . . . smiling. Later, after the evening session, she thrust a piece of paper into my hand. "Thanks!" she whispered.

Later in my room, I read what Carrie had written: "Kathy, after speaking with you, I went down to the river to pray. I told God that for the last time I was going to ask for His forgiveness, and then *let it go.* Then I did a sort of ceremony. I took the cup of tea I was drinking and said, 'Jesus, this tea represents my sin and this river represents You.' Then I threw the rest of my tea into the river. And you know what I noticed? The tea was immediately washed away! There wasn't a trace of it anywhere! Isn't Jesus wonderful?! Thank you for introducing me to Him—again." I was thrilled to read about Carrie's newfound freedom from guilt.

If you are holding yourself captive because you can't forgive yourself for some past sin, God wants you to know that you can drop your sin into the river of His forgiveness and grace. His love is sufficient and He guarantees that the stain will be washed away. He wants you to leave the past behind and press on to a bright future.

That principle of "letting go and letting God" also applies to our next chapter's theme: allowing God to change other people instead of trying to control them ourselves. At times, it's a difficult choice to stop manipulating and release our anger, but God is more powerful than we are in working in the lives of those we love.

⁑*Questions*⁑

1. Which of the results of bitterness listed on pages 143-144 seem the most damaging to you? Which ones have you experienced?

2. Review Proverbs 18:19, which describes being "offended." How does being offended to the point of bitterness make a person "unyielding"? Why do you think that happens?

3. Read Philippians 3:13-14 again. Have you believed that the Bible's command to forget the past means to no longer remember it? Were your efforts to forget successful?

4. Consider the benefits of remembering the past listed on pages 146-147. Which one(s) have you experienced? Which one(s) do you still want to see exhibited in your life?

5. Review 2 Corinthians 1:3-4. How do those verses . . .

- comfort you?
- strengthen you?
- give you direction?

6. Can you think of a time when you were able to comfort someone in a heartfelt way because of your experience of God's
comfort in a similar situation? If so, write about your suffering
and the compassion God created within you because of it.

7. What changes would you like to make in order to become free
from the past and "press on" in Christ? From the following
list, check any that could help:

   ☐ getting professional Christian counseling
   ☐ attending a Christian support group
   ☐ asking one person or a group to pray for you and hold
   you accountable
   ☐ memorizing a Scripture verse or passage
   ☐ refusing to dwell on the past negatively and instead
   acknowledge God's hand in it

8. If the past has created bitterness, whom do you need to forgive? Will you call that person or write a letter expressing your
forgiveness, even if you don't feel like it? Why or why not?

9. If you need to forgive yourself, what step will you take?
Consider having a ceremony similar to Carrie's.

9

Surrender

I will let God change others
as I influence them.

When you seek to play the role of the Holy Spirit in another person's life, you will misdirect that person's battle with God onto yourself.

NEIL ANDERSON

Someone will never hit bottom and look up if we keep putting a pillow underneath them.

WYNETTE HAMMER

$\mathcal{A}$FTER LARRY AND I HAD BEEN MARRIED FOR SEVEN YEARS, we were completely disillusioned with each other. I couldn't understand why Larry didn't love me anymore. He certainly was far from being the Prince Charming I'd married. *Oh Lord, what's wrong with him?* I moaned. *What's wrong with me? I thought we were going to have a perfect marriage because You brought us together. But now we're such strangers, we might as well be divorced.*

I'd tried everything to restore intimacy between us, but nothing seemed to work. The very character qualities that had attracted me to him when we were dating were now the sources of irritation in our relationship. Why did I ever think his ambitiousness and opinionated attitudes were charming?

One morning Larry announced he was flying to San Jose for the day. I quickly suggested, "I'll get the kids ready and we'll go with you."

Larry interrupted me. "Kathy, I'm sorry, but you can't go. I rented a two-seater plane and I've already asked Joe to go with me."

"But Larry, we never see you. Can't you stay home just this once? You're either flying or working so many hours."

"Now, Kathy, I've already explained that I'm working all those hours to secure our financial future. You just don't appreciate all I'm doing for this family."

My face grew hot with fury. "Money isn't helping me cope with these kids!" I snapped. "Darcy makes me so angry sometimes." I didn't have the courage to tell him I was physically abusing her. After all, he was a policeman. Would he have to arrest me?

"Kathy, that's just typical motherhood blues. You'll be fine. I've got to go now."

Larry walked away down the hall as I stood with my hands on my hips, trying to show my disapproval with a disgusted look on my face. I felt like screaming, "Why don't you love me anymore?"

He walked through the laundry room into the garage, closing the laundry room door behind him. To me it was as if he'd slammed it in my face. I had been eating an apple as our conversation started and, before I realized it, my hand with the half-eaten apple pulled back behind my ear and sent it flying toward that door. The apple shattered on impact and hundreds of red and white apple pieces flew throughout the laundry room, adhering to the ceiling and the walls. I whirled around and marched into my bedroom, dropping to kneel beside my bed. "Lord, make that plane crash! I don't care if he ever comes home again."

Larry's plane didn't crash, but I felt as if my life had crashed . . . crashed into a pit of uncontrollable anger and depression. *If only I could make him see how much he's hurting me,* I thought. *If only I could make him stay home more . . . if only I could force him to do what I want him to do . . . then I could be happy.* I was trying to control Larry through my anger. It didn't work.

In time, God healed our misunderstandings and our need to manipulate each other to do things our own ways. As we worked on our disagreements and recommitted our love to each other, God helped us correct our earthly perspective. We began to understand and cooperate with a heavenly viewpoint that says only God can change or control someone else. We certainly can share our opinions and feelings, but we cannot change someone else's. God is the only person who has that power.

While we're in the midst of our anger and our need to manipulate, it's hard to sort through our feelings and thought patterns. But as I look back on that time of hurt and anger in my marriage, I can evaluate what went wrong and identify some common sources of fuel for my controlling behavior. First, I felt threatened. I also thought I knew best, and that if I just nagged enough, I'd get my way.

Feeling Threatened

Trying to control others frequently occurs when we're afraid that someone or something we value is in danger, or a need of ours is being ignored. We want to protect ourselves from hurt and loss.

One of the elements that was influencing the defensive and angry responses between Larry and me was the different ways we looked at life because of our sex. As a woman, I valued our intimacy and didn't want anything to distract from it. Seeing that Larry's two jobs and his hobby appeared to detract from our wedded bliss, I attacked what I perceived to be threatening our relationship. Because I wasn't trusting God or trusting Larry's love for me, I responded like a mother bear anxious to protect her cubs. But my reaction was only perceived by Larry as criticism of his choices.

On the other hand, from his male perspective, Larry was intent on providing for his family through hard work. He was proud of his sacrifice in working two jobs. And he felt he deserved the relief of his flying hobby. He never set out to hurt me, he was just valuing different goals and ideals. From his perspective, a close relationship (which I defined as spending lots of time together) was of secondary importance because of his desire to get ahead financially for the sake of his family. Larry and I now realize that my security (a woman's primary emphasis) was being threatened and his significance (a man's primary goal) was being endangered. We each reacted out of our pain and hurt, believing the other person intentionally wanted to harm us.

Are you feeling threatened in some way? Is something you consider important in danger? Does it make you want to try to control someone or something in order to combat the threat? You may be complaining to the principal about your son's teacher because she isn't teaching him in a way he can learn. You have every right to do that—and you should—but if you're doing it in anger and with the idea that you can control the teacher's philosophy, you're not trusting God to work out His perfect will in His own way.

Maybe you think your position in your company is being threatened by a new employee. Instead of talking to the boss directly about it, you've been talking to your fellow employees and undermining their confidence in the new employee. You think making her look bad will shore up your position. But is that the way God wants you to respond? You can't control the people around you, but you can deal with the situation directly and then work your best to show yourself an exemplary and needed employee.

When we feel threatened, we need to step back and understand that nothing we value can truly be threatened because God is in control and He can empower us to respond in a godly manner. Believing that by faith will help us to release our need to control or change another person.

"I Know Best!"

A second reason we try to control others is because we really believe we know what's best for them. As wife, friend, mother, grandmother, or mentor, we may truly believe we know what is right and good for someone else. Such a belief can create a desire to force that "right" onto that person—but most often when he or she doesn't regard the situation the same way we do. Only God knows the total picture. God looks at the heart. He knows His plans for each person. You and I cannot know all that. We only see in a mirror dimly, but God understands everything about the situation and the way He created that person's perspective.

Plus, we need to realize that our strong opinions are sometimes only reflections of our personality or temperament. One of the keys to Larry's and my healing was learning about the basic human temperaments and the way they cause us to think and behave differently. For us, such knowledge gave understanding and continues to empower us to accept each other and other people unconditionally. Here is a short description of the four basic temperaments identified by many different psychologists and business people who have studied how different people interact.

The Expressive is the person whose main goal in life is to have fun. Expressives love people, excitement, and adventure. They thrive on the compliments and applause of others and are natural speakers who can enthrall one or twenty while they tell a story in grand detail and humor.

The Driver is the person who naturally has a strong opinion and believes his job in life is to control himself, others, and life. Drivers are leaders who can make instant decisions without second-guessing themselves. What bothers everyone else is that often they are right!

The Analytical is the natural perfectionist who strives to make correct decisions and has lofty ideals. Analyticals are more serious-minded as a result, and tend to analyze their own behavior and the actions of others.

The Amiable personality values peace above all else, and sometimes, at all costs. Their energy and enthusiasm are limited and they don't like to "rock the boat" with controversy or strong opinions. The Amiable likes to go along with the crowd and doesn't really have strong ideas anyway, so why not?

Of course, none of us is purely one temperament, and each of the temperaments has its own strengths and weaknesses. Only Jesus—combination of all four temperaments' strengths and none of the weaknesses—can achieve the perfection that the Analytical in all of us craves. Only He can give the perfect direction the Driver aspires to. Only He can bring the joy the Expressive lives for and the peace the Amiable sacrifices herself for.

Because we often marry an opposite temperament and may have children who either are the opposite or the same temperament (and that can be worse sometimes), we are all constantly challenged to respond to someone who views life through a different set of glasses. Even the unmarried person finds relationships a challenge because she is naturally drawn to befriend those who represent the strengths that complement her own weaknesses. In all our deep relationships and connections, we are often subconsciously look-ing for those who complement our weaknesses. If we don't recognize the value of that complementing, we will try to force that other person to look at life the way we do and respond in the way we would in his or her circumstances. In those moments, our own favored perspective makes us think that other person has an earthly perspective, when actually he or she may be looking at life through God's eyes—and we aren't.

My friend and fellow speaker Arlene Kaiser highlights this truth when she writes, "I was eagerly shopping for a unique dress en-semble for a speaking engagement. As I only wear brightly colored, unusual clothes, I knew the task might be difficult. As my eyes scanned the boutique filled with dramatically designed clothes, I noticed a label dangling from the sleeve of most of the garments. The label read, 'This garment is designed of the finest fabric. All nubs, irregular designs are part of the unique fabric and are not a defect of workmanship or material. For best results wash in cold water or dry clean.'

"I surveyed the dress shop crowded with customers and sales-people. They were different sizes, shapes, coloring, and ages. I was reminded of the biblical principle that God creates each one of us unique, a designer creation! I giggled to myself. Imagine God writ-ing a label for every person to wear. It might read, 'Dear Reader: This individual was created with selected characteristics of the finest quality. All marks, slight irregularities, wrinkles, variations of size or color, unexpected behavior or response, in no way should be taken as defects, rather as the unique qualities of this individual. For best results, please learn the care and self-esteem building for this unique individual.'

"As people continue to parade through my life, I imagine each person wearing that label. Just remembering this gives me the insight to be more respectful, kind, and thoughtful of my fellow human beings."[1]

Arlene's point is that "different isn't necessarily wrong," and as we allow people to fulfill their God-given direction, we'll feel less compelled to control and change them. There's a story making the rounds on the Internet entitled "Pastor Search Committee Report." A church, looking for a pastor, investigated many candidates and they just happen to be people from the Bible. Yet, for each one, the committee has found something inadequate based on the external.

> "Noah: He has 120 years of preaching experience, but no converts."
> "Moses: He stutters; and his former congregation says he loses his temper over trivial things."
> "Jeremiah: He is too emotional, alarmist; some say a real 'pain in the neck.'"
> Many others are examined and then Judas is listed with this description: "He seemed to be very practical, cooperative, good with money, cares about the poor, and dresses well. We all agreed that he is just the man we are looking for to fill the vacancy as our Senior Pastor."

When we only look at the external, like that committee did, we may make a very serious mistake. Although only God can look at a person's heart, with His divine understanding we can be understanding while expressing our opinions and ideas appropriately.

Of Course Nagging Works!

A third cause of our need to change or control others could be believing nagging really works! Of course, we may not label it nagging but that really is what we're doing. We focus on the negative and complain, believing that it will motivate someone to do something or make a change in his or her thinking or behavior. But focusing on the negative is a part of an earthly perspective that just doesn't work. Few of us are motivated by it. Rather, we are changed through positive encouragement and an inspiring example of a godly life. A loving influence will have power that complaining and whining never will.

Paul wrote about this when he said in Philippians 2:14: "Do all things without grumbling or disputing." "Grumbling," also interpreted as complaining, is the same word used to describe the Israelites' attitude during their wilderness wanderings. "Disputing" is also interpreted as arguing and carries the idea of "inward questionings." Author Lloyd John Ogilvie says this is "more than healthy intellectual debate, but questioning another person's integrity with suspicion or doubt."[2] Author John F. Walvoord gives an important insight when he writes, "One of the most common failures of Christians who have lost sight of the wonder of God's grace is the tendency to complain, often about simple things such as food and drink, as illustrated in the children of Israel in the wilderness. Such complaining, however, is a symptom of a deep-seated spiritual problem—failure to really trust God and failure to be submissive to His providential provision."[3]

When we're grumbling and disputing about others, we have indeed forgotten the grace of God that forgave us our own sins. Instead of passing that wonderful grace along to others, we find ways to criticize and complain. At those times, we are a poor representation of the Lord to others, especially unbelievers.

When Paul addressed the conflict between Euodia and Syntyche in Philippians 4:2, he first encouraged a fellow believer to help them and then he instructed everyone in verses 4 and 5, "Rejoice in the Lord always; again I will say, rejoice! Let your forbearing spirit be known to all men. The Lord is near." Rejoicing is choosing to focus on the good in a situation. It is appreciating the positive efforts of others even if they don't fulfill all of our expectations. It's also having faith in the Lord's ability to change the other person from the inside out. In a marriage, it's expressing appreciation that your husband put the dishes in the dishwasher even though he didn't wipe off the counter. In parenting, it's giving approval for the "A" even though there's also a "C" on the report card. In friendship, it's not mentioning that a gift is exactly like something you already have. In ministry, it's saying "thank you" for the efforts of the decorating committee even though the result was less than you envisioned.

Nagging doesn't achieve God's purposes or get us the results we want. Instead, we need to be what Paul calls "forbearing," which means reasonable, gentle, big-hearted. So much of what we struggle with in relationships is over the slight and unimportant things: not being taken to dinner, not being given the attention we think we deserve, not being thanked for our efforts. We need to ask ourselves, "Is it really a big deal? Will we think of this ten years from now? In the light of God's kingdom and service to God, is it important?" Most of the time, we are "chewing our cud" on things that are actually insignificant and won't be remembered months later, much less in eternity.

Keeping an eternal perspective helps us to remember that the dissatisfaction we experience in our relationships here on earth won't be remembered in heaven. We can release our need to control and change because we'll each be perfect in heaven. That doesn't mean we won't ever verbally express our dissatisfaction to our husband, child, friend, or family member, but if we're feeling resentful, then we're no longer trusting God; we're trying to take things into our own hands.

We Can't Force Anyone to Change

When we try to take things into our own hands, we're in the most trouble. We cannot force anyone else to change. It's absolutely impossible. Of course, we'll discipline and train our children, but they still have the option of making unwise choices—and many do. We can certainly influence other people, but only God's Holy Spirit can directly change a heart attitude.

Not even Jesus ever forced anyone to change while He lived on earth. He responded to many thousands of people during His time of ministry, but never did He force someone to have a different opinion. He inspired, encouraged, exhorted, and entreated them, but He never coerced them to alter their opinions or beliefs.

Nowhere is that more clear than in Jesus' interaction with the woman at the well, described in John 4:1-42. Jesus gently tries to draw her attention to spiritual freedom but He doesn't force her to accept it. Instead, He sees her inner need and offers her living water.

But the woman is resistant! She counters with, "But drawing water requires something to draw it with! You don't have anything in your hands. Who do you think you are?"

Jesus again tries to remove her earthly lens by telling her once more that she doesn't ever need to be spiritually thirsty again. She can have the water of eternal life.

Now, that sounds good to her. She wants it . . . so that she won't have to come to the well again! She doesn't want water for her soul; she wants her own private well in her own kitchen (then she won't have to walk so far)! She knows she's needy but she can't keep her eyes off her dusty, earthly needs.

Thankfully, Jesus knows her more important needs and quickly goes for the spiritual jugular. "Go, call your husband," He says.

She replies she doesn't have a husband. Jesus says, "Yes, that's true . . . in the literal sense of the word but not in the spirit of the truth. You have actually had five husbands and you're not married to the one you're with now."

The woman must have been flabbergasted. A stranger from another area knows everything about her? But she can't give up that easily, and besides, it's too painful to admit her needs or failures. She acknowledges that Jesus must be some kind of prophet and quickly changes the subject to a controversy: The Samaritans worship nearby but the Jews say there's only one place to worship—in Jerusalem. Her focus is again on an earthly perspective: Let's enter into debate over who does things the right way.

With grace and peace, Jesus patiently continues the conversation. The rest of us would have said, "Oh, let's just get to the point:

You need Jesus in your heart!" But Jesus loves this woman unconditionally. She doesn't need to perform to gain His perfect love. He's
willing to work with her as long as it takes. He directs her thinking to true worship: not following the rules or requirements of a
certain place, but having a personal relationship with God. "Forget the manmade rules," He's saying. "Focus instead on God's desire
for worship from the heart."

The woman tries another smoke screen: the Messiah. The Messiah, the Perfect One, will come, she says. And then the man
standing before her claims to be that very One! Out of all the women
in town, out of all the people in the area . . . Jesus reveals Himself
as Messiah and the Lord God to *her*! But even as Jesus reveals Himself, He still doesn't dictate her choice. He patiently and lovingly
reveals truth and a challenge.

The conversation is interrupted as the disciples return. Jesus
doesn't get frustrated with the interference because He knows God's
Spirit is at work. The woman runs away, leaving her water pot—
representing her old viewpoint of life. Is it broken on the ground?
We don't know, but spiritually speaking she won't need a water pot
anymore: She's met the One who will water her soul forevermore.
She left her home that morning only intending to draw water, but
she encountered the living God Who offered her the abundant spiritual water of grace and peace. No longer was she condemned! She
now could view herself as God did: acceptable and loved; valued
and worthy as His creation.

That transformation occurred as Jesus wooed her to Himself in
patient conversation and loving confrontation. If the Son of God
doesn't feel pressured to force a person to make a life and death
choice, why should we? The same power that drew that woman's
heart to God is the same Spirit Who responds to our prayers and
works in the hearts of those we love. He is much more powerful
than we are. Why should we think that our efforts can be more convincing than His work within a heart and mind?

God's Creative Influence

Not only is God more convincing than we will ever be, but He is also much more creative. Nine years ago, I saw God's creativity change lives in our family. I initially believed that God's direction couldn't bring the results I desired, but He showed me He knew best. I wanted to force a rebellious teenager to change, but God wanted to do it His way—from the inside out.

Darcy was that rebellious fifteen-year-old and we had tried to reach out to her many times. She frequently left the house in the evenings yelling at us. She said she couldn't wait until she was eighteen because she hated living with us and wanted out. We were at our wits' end wondering how we should respond because nothing seemed to help.

In the midst of that stress, Larry was diagnosed with melanoma, the deadliest kind of skin cancer. We were worried that his life was in danger and that that possibility could push Darcy into greater anger and emotional separation from us. I questioned God's wisdom. I had finally given up trying to control or change Darcy, but I sure didn't think God's way would work either.

One evening, Larry and I decided we had to talk with her again. Calling her into our bedroom, we asked her to sit in the chair while we sat against the headboard on our bed. As soon as she sat down, she crossed her arms and glared at us, seemingly defying us to break through her cold and distant resolve.

"Darcy, honey, we love you," Larry began. "We want to know what's going on so that we can work through our differences."

Darcy sat immobilized, her face just as impassive as ever. Larry and I looked at each other feeling hopeless and helpless. "Oh, God," I prayed silently. "Please help us. What will get through to her?"

Larry and I continued to talk to our daughter. Then without any explanation, her face softened, her arms came down and she began talking to us. We were thrilled! For forty-five minutes we talked. We could tell God was healing our relationship. Yet, Larry and I shot glances at each other with a look that questioned, "Why is she finally talking with us?" We had no idea.

When we were finished, Darcy stood up and walked over to the bedroom door. She put her hand on the knob, opened it slightly, and then hesitated. She looked back at us with a confused look and said, "I don't know why I'm talking to you like this. . . ." Then as if the reason had occurred to her, she continued, "But I guess it's because Daddy has cancer."

God had used a creative approach that I never would have thought could be effective. The Lord knew that only something as severe as possibly losing her daddy would make this strong-willed teenager see life through different lenses. Larry's cancerous mole was removed and the cancer has not returned. Darcy never returned to that state of rebellion, and today we all have a fantastic adult relationship.

Are you trusting in God's creative influence to break through a loved one's stony heart? Can you believe that God knows the right approach to changing the heart of your boss or coworker? Can you believe that God will allow the appropriate consequences that will change a heart if you'll stop protecting your loved one? God promises us, "'For I know the plans I have for you,' declares the LORD, 'plans to prosper you and not to harm you, plans to give you hope and a future,'" (Jeremiah 29:11, NIV). His plan may not seem right to you, but He knows the heart condition of every person. He's not only working to change the heart of the one you love but your heart as well.

Personal Transformation

As you and I allow God to work in others and in the situations we're tempted to control, we will see changes in our own hearts as well. When we're trying to change and control others, our spiritual vision is focused on them. But God wants to shift our focus back to Him and to transform us through the frustrating experiences we encounter. His work isn't just for other people's good; it's for ours too.

I experienced that truth some time ago after Larry and I made a major purchase from a Christian business. In time, the company informed us they weren't able to supply the item after all and promised a refund. When we didn't receive the refund after repeated requests to the employees and even the president, we realized we were being given the run-around. I was furious. Though the money wasn't a huge amount, it made a difference to us. But what was more aggravating was that this company advertised itself as a Christian business! How dare they operate in an ungodly manner!

I definitely wanted to change this situation. The more I thought about their dishonesty, the angrier I got. Larry and I have always handled our money with the spirit that we are God's stewards and He is the owner of the money He gives us. I couldn't believe that God would want His money treated this way. Certainly He wanted His money where it belonged: in our rightful grasp!

One day as I had my devotions, my thoughts again turned to the situation. Anger boiled up inside of me. I wrote in my journal, "This is a trial and a test of whether we really trust the Lord and believe in His righteousness and justice. How we respond about this will show whether we've truly surrendered our possessions to God. We say we're just stewards, are we going to be owners now?

"That doesn't mean we shouldn't try to do something about it. We should. But more important is our attitude. If we become angry and anxious, that is an indicator that we regard the money as our own. If we trust God for the outcome and indeed emotionally release the money, that's an indicator we regard it as God's loss. And if He wants to lose His money, then that's His business!

"God is righteous and just. He can replace the money in another way if He wants us to have it. If not, He is in charge of the judgment of others. My anger—which wells up in me as we place fruitless and impotent phone calls— can be replaced by trust in the Lord. Praise the Lord!"

I took several deep breaths and sensed the Lord wanting me to again release this whole situation to Him. I continued writing. "Father God, this is not hidden from Your sight and neither are Your eyes closed and uncaring. Thank you, Lord, that I can surrender all my cares to You."

Even though I had made a choice to trust, my emotions weren't following my mind's lead too closely. I still felt like I wanted to control the situation. So I decided to find a verse to memorize so that, when my anger started to boil again, I could meditate on that verse. I flipped through the New Testament trying to find an appropriate verse, but the Lord seemed to whisper in my heart, "Look at Jeremiah 17." I argued, "Lord, you know I'm memorizing those verses and there's nothing in that passage that applies to this situation." I again turned my Bible's pages but nothing stood out. When the Holy Spirit repeated His message about Jeremiah, I surrendered. "Okay, Father, but You know there's nothing there."

I turned to Jeremiah 17 and, at the top of that page, a verse that I'd marked in yellow many years earlier caught my eye. I read Jeremiah 16:17: "For My eyes are on all their ways; they are not hidden from My face, nor is their iniquity concealed from My eyes." I couldn't believe it. Those were some of the very words I'd just written in my journal. It was as if God were telling me in a striking way that He truly was aware and would do His will.

In that moment, a calm came over me and I had a deep sense of trust in God's plan. Suddenly I could look at this whole situation from an eternal perspective, rather than an earthly one. In time, we did receive the refund we were due, but God had already done the important part: He helped me to see through His eyes.

Is someone you're trying to influence resisting your efforts? Could it be that God not only wants to make a difference in his or her life but in yours as well? Maybe that talkative woman keeps coming to your Bible study because God wants you to learn to be a better listener. Perhaps your toddler's disobedience can teach you how important it is to be more consistent in applying consequences. What heart attitude in *you* is God desiring to change? What behavior is He saying to modify? Your circumstances may not change until *you* change.

But in the meantime, be assured that God wants only the best for you. Just as Jesus patiently drew the woman at the well closer to His loving heart, He'll do the same for you.

That's exactly what God was doing in my life when He didn't immediately answer my prayer for Larry to change his ways. My angry efforts at manipulation, nagging, and control totally failed. I left the rotting pieces of apple adhered to the walls and ceiling of my laundry room as a memorial to the rotten marriage I believed God could not or would not change.

But then God began to do a work within my own heart. He convicted me of my sin of trying to control Larry and all of life. He revealed the underlying earthly perspective that made me think Larry was responsible for my happiness. Through prayer, reading books, Bible study, and asking other women to hold me accountable for my own growth, I began to view my situation in a different light. My vision was corrected when I realized I couldn't change Larry, I could only change myself as I surrendered to God.

On the day I began to see myself and my situation through God's eyes, I went into the laundry room and washed off those rotting apple pieces. I no longer needed a memorial to my rotten marriage. I needed to wash the rotten attitudes off my heart and mind and to trust God with my marriage and my life.

In some aspect of your life, are you waiting for someone else to change so that you can live the life you know you should? Does your anger feel justified because you think it's the appropriate way to communicate your displeasure? Do you think you are better at changing a person than the Spirit of God is? Those are the elements of an earthly perspective. Choose an eternal perspective instead and give up trying to change or control someone else. You can't change others, but God can change you. And that may be the first step to Him working in the other person's heart as well.

In our next chapter, we'll examine something closely related to this issue of releasing control: learning the eternal perspective of choosing contentment regardless of circumstances.

⸙ *Questions* ⸙

1. What person or situation do you feel compelled to change or control? Why do you feel a need to do that? Consider the reasons given on page 160 or come up with your own.

2. Review the descriptions of the basic temperaments on page 162. How would you describe your temperament? What are the temperaments of the people you love or those you deal with daily?

3. How does understanding the basic temperaments you're dealing with help you to release control over someone?

4. Review Philippians 2:14. How does the "grumbling" and "disputing" described resemble nagging?

5. Do you think nagging works? Can you think of a time it actually did?

6. What current situation is tempting you to nag? How can you resist the temptation?

7. Read Philippians 4:1-5. Using your imagination, list some of the possible conflicts Euodia and Syntyche might have experienced to draw them apart. In each of those situations, consider how a fellow Christian like the one Paul mentioned in Philippians 4:3 could have helped.

8. How is Paul's appeal to rejoice in Philippians 4:4 a solution for conflict? How have you seen rejoicing bring peace into a potential difficulty?

9. What do you think Paul meant when he used the word "forbearing" (Philippians 4:5)?

10. Could Paul's exhortation to be "forbearing" assist you in allowing God to change others? How?

11. Review the account of Jesus and the woman at the well in John 4:1-42. In what ways are you like the woman?

12. What do you learn from Jesus' behavior in this story about responding to others without trying to control them?

13. How have you seen God creatively work in the lives of others? In yourself? How does that demonstrate God's promise in Jeremiah 29:11?

14. In what specific ways might God want to use the difficult relationships in your life to change you for the better?

Contentment

I can choose to be content
regardless of circumstances.

For peace of mind, resign as general manager of the universe.

LARRY EISENBERG

A man who suffers before it is necessary suffers more than is necessary.

LUCIUS ANNAEUS SENECA

I HEARD THE NEIGHBORS PLAYING AND LAUGHING IN THEIR POOL AND thought, *Now that's what I want on a Father's Day. A family playing together in a pool.*

We had the pool, but no one wanted to be in it. Darcy and Mark were playing at neighbors' houses, Larry was lying on the couch watching football, and I moped around the house disgruntled. I felt like my family was falling apart.

Discontent crept over me until tears stung my eyes. "Why can't things be different?" I wanted to scream. "Why can't our family be closer, especially on Father's Day?" Though I had grown tremendously in my ability to be content over the years since God had healed me of abusive anger, I was convinced I could no longer choose to be content. I just didn't have the emotional energy. Everything seemed of major importance and I felt overwhelmed.

I escaped to the bedroom, knelt by the bed, and poured out my discontent to the Lord. After releasing my frustration, I slowly began to see that even though I didn't have the strength to choose to be content, the Lord could empower me as I made a choice to obey Him. I prayed, "Lord, please empower me to trust You for all these dissatisfying circumstances. I give thanks for the progress that has been made in my marriage and family. I renew my commitment to trust You for the changes You want. Thank You. I love You. Amen."

I then decided to do what I could to embrace contentment. I set the table with china and silver for a special dinner that would bring the family together for at least a short time. Busying myself with this act of love eventually caused my discontent to slip away. The day wasn't to my preference in every way, but at least I had received God's power to make one small step to arranging some together-ness—and to experiencing some inner peace.

Discontentment Is Everywhere

We are a dissatisfied society. And the media both reflect and per-
petuate our discontent by ever reminding us that we have not
"arrived." We should want to climb the corporate ladder and have
the latest computer, software, and toaster. We should be dissatisfied with our paycheck, possessions, even our friends (or our
husband) if they don't make us happy. Some people seek multiple
college degrees and place primary importance on education. Many
of us base our contentment on how much weight we've lost or
whether we can run a marathon. And if we've conquered a
marathon, then triathlons beckon us. We want endless variety in
our eating, drinking, dressing, decorating, working, and playing.

Another form of discontentment is pining for the magical day
when all our desires will be met and our problems solved. Many
years ago, I invited a neighbor to our women's neighborhood Bible
study and she replied, "As soon as I get my problems solved, I'll
come." She had a form of discontentment that said, "When everything is good in my life, I'll do other things." That woman divorced
her husband and abandoned her daughter. But she couldn't find
contentment after making those unwise choices, either.

If we're not content, we're continually looking for the next high
that will bring us fulfillment. But only God satisfies completely. We
can try to cram our spirit with other things of this world, but only
His presence penetrates the void. Author A. W. Tozer wrote, "When
religion has its last word, there is little that we need other than God
Himself. The evil habit of seeking 'God—and' effectively prevents
us from finding God in full revelation. In the 'and' lies our great woe.
If we omit the 'and' we shall soon find God, and in Him we shall
find that for which we have all our lives been secretly longing."[1]

In Job 36:11 we're told that obedience brings prosperity and
contentment. Psalm 17:15 tells how the psalmist found satisfaction
through being in God's presence. Psalm 36:5 indicates that prais-
ing God brings a satisfied feeling. Psalm 90:14 sings, "Satisfy us

in the morning with your unfailing love, that we may sing for joy and be glad all our days"(NIV). Ecclesiastes says that it's good to find satisfaction in our work because it's a gift of God. But without a focus on God while we work, that gift becomes meaningless. Ecclesiastes also tells us that money never satisfies.

No wonder people who don't know Christ have a deep discontent. That spiritual hole in their hearts is being filled only with small portions of "things." Those earthly things pale in comparison with the joy and fulfillment of knowing God personally and experiencing His love, acceptance, and approval.

A Biblical View on Contentment

Many people think they can never achieve contentment because they can't imagine being happy about all situations they might face. There is hope for them because contentment is not the same as being happy.

Happiness is an emotion that results from pleasant circumstances. It's very "fickle" and can appear and disappear depending upon what's going on in our lives. It doesn't require any choice on our part. Contentment, on the other hand, is an active trusting in God that may or may not be expressed with an outward happiness. Being content means choosing to believe that God is in control of all my circumstances, regardless of how life appears.

But making that choice can be hard. My friend Neva B. True has shared with me how difficult it was for her to find contentment in her early adult years. She kept trying to find it by being happy. She says, "I tried to find contentment in many things: a job change for my husband, a move to a better house with coordinated furniture, an attractive wardrobe, and perfect kids. I thought finding those things would bring contentment into my life. Only through the Lord's grace has He convinced me that 'a tent or a cottage, why should I care; they're building a mansion for me over there.' Now I don't depend upon happiness for my contentment. I've learned that it comes from Jesus." Neva has learned a valuable lesson. Happiness is something that happens to you, but contentment is something we choose.

When we think of that kind of contentment as represented in the Bible, most of us think of Paul's writing in Philippians 4:11-13: "I am not saying this because I am in need, for I have learned to be content whatever the circumstances. I know what it is to be in need, and I know what it is to have plenty. I have learned the secret of being content in any and every situation, whether well fed or hungry, whether living in plenty or in want. I can do everything through him who gives me strength" (NIV).

As I researched the word "contentment" as expressed in that verse, I was surprised to learn that Paul actually used the Greek word *autarkēs,* which means "entirely self-sufficient." Autarkeia was the highest aim of the Stoics of Paul's time, and to them it meant the state of mind of a person who has completely divorced himself from feeling any desire, pain, or joy. The Stoics wanted nothing to be important to them and practiced saying "I don't care" when anything happened, good or bad. But their goal was so extreme that a person who had achieved their brand of "contentment" could watch his most beloved relative or friend suffer pain and die, and yet say, "I don't care." Unfortunately, they supported this philosophy through a wrong application of accepting God's will.

How wonderful that this isn't the kind of contentment God wants us to have! Paul arrived at a different kind of *autarkēs*—contentment—through recognizing that God would strengthen him to choose to be happy regardless of his circumstances, as he expressed in verse 13. Commentator William Barclay underlines the difference between Paul and the Stoics by commenting, "The Stoic said, 'I will learn content by a deliberate act of my own will.' Paul said, 'I can do all things through Christ who infuses his strength into me.' For the Stoic contentment was a human achievement; for Paul it was a divine gift. The Stoic was self-sufficient; but Paul was God-sufficient. Stoicism failed because it was inhuman; Christianity succeeded because it was rooted in the divine. Paul could face anything, because in every situation he had Christ; the man who walks with Christ can cope with anything."[2]

But Paul didn't instantly arrive at this state of contentment the moment he encountered Jesus. As he says, he "learned" it. How comforting for us to know that even the great apostle Paul had to go through a process of learning to be content! Contentment doesn't come easily for any of us. As you and I see our circumstances, problems, and trials through God's eyes, we will learn to be content through whatever landscapes God leads us.

The Fuel of Discontent

How can we make that choice for contentment? By identifying the attitudes that feed our discontent. One of the most powerful fuels is worry. In the same chapter where Paul describes his journey toward contentment, he also writes about worry and anxiety. Worry feeds dissatisfaction because it makes us focus on what we're afraid will happen.

A mother may stay awake at night, restlessly alert to every siren because her daughter is out on a date. A policeman's wife may listen all night to the scanner, fearing her husband is in danger while on duty. All this thinking and concentration doesn't alter circumstances, but somehow it feels like we're doing something to protect our loved one.

Luke 12:29-31 in the *Phillips* translation commands us: "You must not set your heart on what you eat or drink, nor must you live in a state of anxiety. The whole heathen world is busy about getting food and drink, and your Father knows well enough that you need such things. No, set your heart on his kingdom, and your food and drink will come as a matter of course." God doesn't want us to be anxious. He knows our needs and desires. Yet, how easy it is to be fearful that our needs won't be met, or that our loved ones won't be protected, or that bad things will happen.

Someone has said, "Worry is like a rocking chair. It gives you something to do but you don't go anywhere." How true! Our minds whirl with fear, yet worry never helps. Someone recently told me a different perspective, though. She said, "Of course worry helps. Whenever I worry about something, it doesn't happen!" I hope she meant that tongue-in-cheek, although she actually spoke the truth: Most of the time we worry about what will never happen. Not because we worried but because it wasn't going to happen anyway!

The English word "worry" comes from the German word *wurgen*, meaning "to strangle, to choke." When worry rules our minds and hearts, it does feel as if we are being strangled. And worry definitely chokes out our ability to trust God. Author Charles Swindoll asks, "What qualifies as a worry? Anything that drains your tank of joy—something you cannot change, something you are not responsible for, something you are unable to control, something (or someone) that frightens and torments you, agitates you, keeps you awake when you should be asleep. All of that now needs to be switched from your worry list to your prayer list."[3]

Worry is merely our minds casting away the truth of God's love and goodness. If we truly believe He loves us, we won't worry because He cares about us. If we truly believe God is good, we won't worry because we know He gives us the best. Our difficulty is in the definition of "the best." We humans believe it means only experiencing things that make us happy. But from an eternal perspective, God says bad things will happen because we live in a fallen world. He also promises to provide opportunities for us to grow through those difficult circumstances.

The Antidote for Worry

Paul's primary antidote for worry is prayer: "Be anxious for nothing, but in everything by prayer and supplication with thanksgiving let your requests be made known to God" (Philippians 4:6). Worry doesn't accomplish anything but prayer does!

One of my most memorable experiences of how prayer relieves worry occurred some time ago when Larry was on duty. He was still a cop on the beat and although God has always given me a peace about his job, there are times when worry can seize my mind with fear. One evening, I felt that fear begin to grab hold. At the same time, I sensed the Lord saying, "Pray for Larry!" I'd never sensed that so strongly, and I dropped to my knees beside my bed and prayed for his safety. After several minutes, I felt at peace and went to bed with a calm heart.

Larry arrived home after his swing shift and I woke up. He began telling me about how he had gone to a call where a woman was holding her mother-in-law hostage. She was threatening her with a gun and wanted to find her husband so she could kill him. As Larry and three fellow officers approached the door talking to her, the mother-in-law suddenly jumped the woman and wrestled her to the ground. Larry and the officers ran in knowing the gun could go off any moment. It did—several times. They were able to take control of the situation and wrestle the woman into surrender. They were amazed to discover that no one had been shot . . . all the bullets ended up in the walls of the apartment.

I was wide awake by then and asked Larry what time that had happened. He gave me the exact time I'd been praying for his safety.

My worry could not have helped Larry but my prayers for his safety, directed by God, protected him and gave me peace. I've never been impressed to pray like that since and Larry has never been in as dangerous a situation.

The next time you're tempted to worry, pray instead! It may be God's cue that your loved one needs His protection or strength. By praying and trusting God, you'll find a deep level of contentment, knowing you don't have to be dissatisfied with God's work: He knows what He's doing.

When worry is bombarding us, it's often hard to remember the antidote of prayer. That's why as I teach about coping with worry during seminars and retreats, I pass out file cards and I share a tip

I originally heard from H. Norman Wright. I have everyone write in big letters on one side of the card, "STOP." On the other side, they write out Philippians 4:5-6. They are to carry this card with them and whenever they begin to worry, pull it out, say out loud, "Stop!" and then read Philippians 4:5-6 to themselves: "Kathy, be anxious for nothing, and so on." I've heard from several women who have seen God use that card as a means of reducing worry. It's just about impossible to worry and simultaneously turn your attention to the Lord.

Paul also commands us to include thanksgiving in our prayers. Giving thanks diminishes worry and builds contentment by rehearsing God's faithfulness in the past.

I'm amazed at how many of the Psalms are a reminder of God's work in the past. Psalm 111:1-4 is a good example:

Praise the LORD!
I will give thanks to the LORD with all my heart,
In the company of the upright and in the assembly.
Great are the works of the LORD;
They are studied by all who delight in them.
Splendid and majestic is His work;
And His righteousness endures forever.
He has made His wonders to be remembered;
The LORD is gracious and compassionate.

When I rehearse what God has done for me in the past, I can face today's fear-producing circumstances with far less anxiety. God knows the plan He has in mind; therefore, I can be content in spite of what I fear could happen.

Lloyd John Ogilvie says, "I used to ask, worry, and ask again as if God were hard of hearing. Now I am trying to learn how to ask once and thank him repeatedly."[4] Rehearsing His faithfulness in the past will enable us to do that.

The next time you're worried that something terrible is going to happen to your children, focus on God's protection of them in the past. The next time you're worried that you'll be downsized out of your job, focus on God's provision of a job in the past. The next time you're worried that you will face illness, focus on God's ability to strengthen you like the previous times you faced difficulty. As you do, you'll experience the peace that God promises in Philippians 4:7: "And the peace of God, which surpasses all comprehension, shall guard your hearts and your minds in Christ Jesus."

Perfect Peace

God's peace surpasses our comprehension because it's something we can't manufacture on our own. It's a gift from God. Peace "guards" our hearts and minds like a sentry. The Greek word for guard is *phrourein,* a military word for "standing on guard." Author Kenneth S. Wuest says, "God's peace, like a sentinel, mounts guard and patrols before the heart's door, keeping worry out."[5]

Envision it this way, based on the principle of 2 Corinthians 10:5, that "we are taking every thought captive to the obedience of Christ." Your heart is being bombarded by worry. Arrows of thought labeled, "What if . . . " and "If that happens . . . " are targeted at the very center of your soul. You recognize one of the arrow's labels, a familiar one: "What if my children rebel when they are teenagers? Since I'm not doing a very good job as a mother, they will most likely hate me when they grow up." This arrow is a very sharp one and you have succumbed to it frequently in the past. "O Lord, I'm not going to fall for this again," you decide. "I can't control my children's future responses, but I can be the best mom I can be right now. I'm going to sign up at church for that parenting class. Please help me in my reactions, and thank You for the good relationship the kids and I have right now."

God's sentinel, assigned at the door of your heart as a result of prayer, praise, and thanksgiving, steps forward and grabs the arrow right before it enters your heart. He flings it away, having taken it captive to the obedience of Christ. As it hurtles away, it shrinks. It will be even easier for the sentinel to take it captive next time.

Another arrow is in the air, headed straight for you. It's labeled, "If I lose my job, how will I support my family?" You pray, "Lord, I can't control my boss's response to me. All I can do is work hard. If I lose my job because of downsizing, I believe you have something even better for me. I remember when my friend Brent was fired through no fault of his own. He was out of work for a while, but grew closer to You. He says it was a precious time of getting to know You better. Now he has the best job in the world. You can do the same for me. Thank You!"

The sentinel snatches the arrow out of the air, many feet before it can reach your heart. He breaks it over his knee and throws it down. Its power is broken.

Not only do we have this sentinel of peace standing guard because of our prayers and trust in God, but the sentinel is also strengthened by the Holy Spirit, Who prays for us in God's very presence. Romans 8:26 assures us, "And in the same way the Spirit also helps our weakness; for we do not know how to pray as we should, but the Spirit Himself intercedes for us with groanings too deep for words."

As I meditated on that verse two years ago, I was struggling with feelings of inadequacy and discontentment because of the situation I described in an earlier chapter: being canceled as a speaker at an event. I wrote in my journal:

> I decided to light a candle and have it on my desk flickering to remind me of the truth that the Spirit is praying for me in Your very presence, Lord. I can imagine His words. . . .
>
> The Spirit speaks up, "Father, Kathy needs help. She's trying and wanting to live in Our power but she keeps forgetting how powerful We are. She still hasn't fully believed

that We will empower her for the doors We open for her. In fact, she's not totally convinced We've opened these doors."

The Father replies, "I know this has been a problem for a while. I love her so much and I've uniquely designed her ministry just for her but she still can't fully comprehend I can favor her in that way. I know the incident has destroyed some of her confidence but I know this will make her depend on Me rather than on herself. It's not necessary she know why that happened or how, only that I will use it for good."

Jesus replies, "It must be hard for humans who want to know the why and how of everything. But Kathy is growing in her ability to trust Us. And didn't I show her My power last night when she was able to find the verses for her project so quickly? I know all the projects she has. I know exactly how I'll make her time stretch to complete everything. Because she's doing the things You want her to do, Father."

The Spirit interjects, "Father, I'm protecting her—as she turns to Me—from Satan's attacks. She got another one last night when someone reminded her about the cancellation. That has her bummed and frustrated again."

The Father replies, "Satan is crafty, isn't he? Just when she thought she was over the hurt, he opens the wound again. Spirit, make sure she rebukes and resists Satan's fiery doubts and arrows with faith in Our ability to work everything for good."

Spirit: "I think Kathy's doing that more and more. Another layer in her pride is being stripped away."

Father: "Kathy is one of Our many faithful servants. I know her works, her love for Me, her desire to please Me."

Spirit: "I agree. Satan is not going to have his way with her. I know she'll continue to call upon Our power."

All three members of the Trinity nod and smile.

As I continued to journal my thoughts, God's incomprehensible peace took control of my heart. I could be content because I knew that God was in charge of my ministry and my reputation.

Dwelling on the Good

Another way to strengthen your sentinel is found in Philippians 4:8: "Finally, brethren, whatever is true, whatever is honorable, whatever is right, whatever is pure, whatever is lovely, whatever is of good repute, if there is any excellence and if anything worthy of praise, let your mind dwell on these things."

The word "dwell" means "careful reflection." Someone has written:

> Keep your thoughts positive because your thoughts become your words.
>
> Keep your words positive because your words become your actions.
>
> Keep your actions positive because your actions become your habits.
>
> Keep your habits positive because your habits become your values.
>
> Keep your values positive because your values become your identity.

You and I are in a constant battle to dwell on those things that honor God. When we do, contentment is our prize. But when we don't, we slip into an earthly frame of mind. Charles Swindoll said, "These minds of ours are like bank vaults awaiting our deposits. If we regularly deposit positive, encouraging, and uplifting thoughts, what we withdraw will be the same. And the interest paid will be joy."[6] And contentment!

What does verse 8 suggest we concentrate on?

Whatever is true. "True" refers to things that are not a distortion of reality. Satan is the father of lies and loves for us to make wrong, distorted assumptions about life. Some of the lies I've believed in the past include:

- My husband is responsible for my happiness.
- Once I get him past the altar, I'll alter him.
- My children are a reflection of me. If they misbehave, I must be a bad mother.
- If people don't like me, I don't have worth and value.
- I must say "yes" to every request for my attention because that's what a godly woman does.

Those wrong ideas gave birth to stress, anger, resentment, depression, and self-hatred for many years. Captivating those lies and correcting them with the truth continues to set me free.

Whatever is honorable. Commentator William Barclay says this word "describes that which has the dignity of holiness upon it. There are things in this world which are flippant and cheap and attractive to the light-minded; but it is on the things which are serious and dignified that the Christian will set his mind."[7] This certainly isn't suggesting we never have fun, laugh, or enjoy ourselves. We know that joy and laughter are recommended in Scripture. Barclay is referring to the things in this world that are in opposition to God's teachings and pull our minds and hearts in the wrong direction.

My own watching of one particular soap opera didn't exactly meet God's criteria for "that which is honorable." At one point, watching "All My Children" became so important to me that I found myself praying for the characters! I hurt when they hurt and rejoiced when they rejoiced. I thought more about their problems than I did my own. That's not taking every thought captive to the obedience of Christ! Although I no longer watch that program regularly, I'm still tempted at times to turn it on while I eat my lunch. I'm trying to choose to read an inspirational magazine instead. I want to spiritually feed on that which has the "dignity of holiness."

Whatever is right. Whatever is of righteousness and correct living is what God wants us to dwell on. Doing the right thing when society identifies wrong as "right" is desperately needed by the world. Integrity is talked about, but rarely practiced.

Author John Archer documented an example of righteousness in a magazine article. "In 1968, while serving as an Army surgeon in Vietnam," he writes, "Dr. Kenneth Swan labored for seven hours at the operating table to save the life of a nineteen-year-old soldier mangled by an enemy grenade. Other doctors, noting that the young man had lost his legs and his eyesight, ridiculed Swan. 'He would have been better off dead,' they chided.

"Haunted by those words for twenty years, Dr. Swan decided to find out whether his life-saving efforts had been a mistake. After a two-year search, he finally located the injured soldier. The man had a loving wife and two daughters, a good job, a zest for life, and a strong faith in God. None of that would have been possible without Swan's moral courage."[8] Dr. Swan was encouraged when he found good results from his choice to do "right."

Whatever is pure. Just as a cheesecloth filters and separates the edible from the undesirable, our thoughts should filter out that which is pure from the impure. Although we can't prevent thoughts of lust or temptation from heading our way, we can choose to empower our sentinel to intercept them. Those temptations aren't sin until we welcome them into our hearts and accept them as our own.

Whatever is lovely. If a thought encourages us to love others, then let's welcome it and dwell upon it. If a thought feeds bitterness and resentment, then we need to refuse to dwell upon it.

Whatever is of good repute. Various Bible versions translate "good repute" as "gracious," "high-toned," and "whatever has a good name." William Barclay suggests it describes "things which are fit for God to hear."[9] When we choose to dwell on that which is of good repute, we will refuse to gossip and rehearse the hurts others have inflicted upon us.

Whatever is excellent and worthy of praise. Finally, in case anything has been left out, Paul encompasses everything good in his exhortation to dwell on anything excellent and praiseworthy. Does what we're thinking about motivate us to do better and bring glory to God? Then we should dwell on it and let it become a part of us.

What are you filling your bank vault with? Positive or negative deposits? Are you making more withdrawals or deposits? What you put in is going to be the fuel for your journey toward contentment.

God Will Meet All Our Needs

Filling our mental and emotional bank vault with contentment is often sabotaged because of our focus on personal goals and possessions. There have been many times when I've thought, "Once the new drapes get installed, my living room will be complete and I'll be content" or "Once the kids are gone to school all day, then I'll be content" or "When I get my mom's approval, then I'll be at peace." The list goes on and on. The call of what the world gives is like that. These things beckon us, make us discontented, and even if they arrive in our lives, they quickly lose their significance.

Think of something you once wanted very much and then received. Does it still make you happy? Or has it lost its "punch"? Now think of something you once longed for and didn't receive. Have you somehow been able to continue living with joy without it?

The key to you and me being able to find contentment regardless of what we possess is wrapped in the great truth of Philippians 4:19: "My God shall supply all your needs according to His riches in glory in Christ Jesus." We nod our agreement with that verse, but we often don't recognize that we may have a different definition of "needs" than God does. We must learn to see "needs" and "wants" through God's eyes.

Christian psychologist Larry Crabb says, "Because people are both physical beings and personal beings, they have both physical needs and personal needs. Physical needs consist of whatever is needed to physically survive, to keep the body alive—food, clothing, shelter, etc. Personal needs consist of whatever is required to personally survive, to keep the person alive—significance and security as a basis for self-worth."[10]

Crabb says that we must "differentiate between needs and wants. We need significance and security in order to persevere in faithful living. We may want approval, money, fame, recognition, etc., etc. And I may passionately want them to the point where their absence provokes a nonsinful legitimate pain of excruciating proportions. But I do not need any of them in order to be a whole person who can live biblically."[11]

Hebrews 13:5 tells us: "Keep your lives free from the love of money and be content with what you have, because God has said, 'Never will I leave you; never will I forsake you'" (NIV). You and I can be content, free of worry, and equipped to see life through God's eyes because God promises to never abandon us. In whatever we face, we can know He will provide for our true needs, and usually out of His incredible graciousness He provides many of our wants as well.

Can you act on those truths in spite of whatever you're facing right now? Even if your child is sick, there's no need to worry, only pray. Even if you could lose your job, there's no need to dwell on fearful scenarios. Instead, obey God's leading and rest in the fact that He'll never leave you or forsake you. Even if you can't afford that new couch, trust that if God wants you to have it, He'll provide. Make a fresh commitment today to stay focused on contentment.

In our final chapter, we'll wrap up our thoughts on looking at life through God's eyes by focusing on our eternal destination: heaven. What can God's promise for our future do for us today?

✧ *Questions* ✧

1. Why do you think there is so much discontentment in our
   world? In what area of life do you notice it the most?

2. In what area are you most content and in what area are you
   least?

3. Do you worry much or little? Why?

4. How have you seen prayer be an antidote to worry and a
   support for contentment?

5. Create your own "peace" card according to the instructions
   on page 185. Carry it with you and use it when worry begins
   to create tension in your mind.

6. Why do you think it's important to thank God after making a request (Philippians 4:6)? How does gratitude limit the power of worry and help contentment to grow?

7. In what circumstance or area of life do you need to be grateful? How will you do that in one specific way this week?

8. Meditate on the good things God wants us to dwell on as listed in Philippians 4:8. Which one do you enjoy concentrating on most often? Which one is most difficult for you?

9. How will you dwell on the good during the next week? As you do, what change in your thinking or reacting do you anticipate?

10. In what ways are you discontented about what you have or wish you had? What "thing" did you anticipate would give you contentment when you purchased or received it? Did it? What did you learn from that experience?

Transcendence

*I am a citizen of heaven
and I won't be complete until I am
at home with God.*

For the Christian, heaven is not a goal; it is a destination.
The goal is that Christ be formed in you.

RICHARD J. FOSTER

Embracing the reality of the world to come radically
alters everything in this world. Our values are prioritized
and purified. Money, things, time, friends, enemies,
family, and life itself are all adjusted to their appropriate
worth and place.

JOSEPH STOWELL

I FELT REALLY SILLY. HERE IT WAS 88 DEGREES IN SOUTHERN CALI-
fornia and I was adorned with a wool skirt, cotton sweater, wool
blazer, and boots. Over my arm, I'd slung a wool coat. If my neighbors had by chance looked out their windows to see me loading the
car with my luggage, they must have wondered whether I'd lost my
marbles. But the revealing clue to my state of mind is that I was loading luggage! I was on my way to the airport for a flight to the East
Coast where a blizzard was in process. I'd rather be hot here for a
little bit of time and kept warm there the whole time I'm visiting.

As I walked through the airport, most people had on shorts,
T-shirts, and sandals. But some of us who were headed for colder
destinations lugged our warm clothing. It seemed awkward and a
bother to be wearing the bulky clothes and hauling the heavy coats,
but I knew it would pay off when I was bundled up warm in the
freezing wind of New York. And indeed, once I arrived in New York,
I fit right in! Everyone had on their wool clothing and either carried or wore a heavy coat. I didn't feel awkward at all but grateful
for the warmth enveloping me.

As my contact person for my speaking engagement escorted me
to her car, I suddenly recognized the spiritual analogy that my transformation from warm Southern California to freezing New York
communicated. It's the idea expressed in Philippians 3:20-21: "For
our citizenship is in heaven, from which also we eagerly wait for a
Savior, the Lord Jesus Christ; who will transform the body of our
humble state into conformity with the body of His glory, by the exertion of the power that He has even to subject all things to Himself."

You and I are inhabitants of earth but we are citizens of heaven.
We are aliens surrounded by the "hot weather" of an anti-heaven culture, yet our "clothing" is heavenly. We're supposed to be "dressed"

for heaven by looking at our lives, relationships, and challenges with the "warm clothing" of our future eternity. We awkwardly wear our earthly clothing and don't fit in within the culture of immorality, distrust of God, self-dependence, and self-absorption. Our spiritual appetites are strange to those who don't have a passport for heaven, but once we reach our destination and are transformed into our heavenly permanent bodies, our spiritual perspective will seem completely normal.

But since that hasn't happened yet, you and I are challenged to keep an eternal perspective while tempted by this temporary world's fare and frame of reference. Since we're aliens here, you could even say we're homeless. How wonderful to know our Heavenly Father is preparing a mansion fit for His princesses, and one day soon we will transcend all the trappings of earth and thrive in His glorious presence!

Webster's *New World Dictionary* defines alien as "belonging to another country or people; foreign; strange; not natural." A foreigner is "a visitor or resident from another country, especially one with a different language, cultural pattern, etc." As aliens on earth and future citizens of heaven, we're supposed to be distinct from unbelievers around us. We should be exemplifying our "different language and cultural pattern" to all around us. We should be viewing life from an eternal perspective and acting as if we know where we're headed.

Author Joseph Stowell writes, "The pilgrim mind-set, best exemplified by Abraham (see Hebrews 11:8-10), recognizes that as aliens we don't belong here and that we live seeking the country to which we do belong. To claim a pilgrim's identity means that we always know we're not home yet. For us the best is yet to come. Therefore, everything is expendable here, free to be used for the glory and gain of the King.

"Living in the reality of heaven has tremendous relevance. When we envision heaven as our home, everything in life is radically rearranged. It affects our posture toward God, our possessions, people, pain and pleasure. And heaven in our hearts purifies us and alters our sense of identity."[1]

A Heavenly Birth Certificate

When we're born, we're declared "alive" by a birth certificate. When we are "born again," God declares us spiritually alive! Our names are written in His Book of Life and we are given a heavenly birth certificate that assures us our final destination is heaven, our real home. God's eternal claim upon our lives can help us when life on earth becomes overwhelming and dissatisfying because we have hope in knowing all this won't be for nothing. Someday all the pain will be past. And in the meantime, God has a plan.

That truth strengthened me some time ago when I was grieved over the difficulties that have faced my son, Mark, since elementary school. Because of a learning disability and low-key personality, Mark has always struggled academically and in coping with life. He faced constant failure, never having a sense of success as he barely made grade-level scores in school. Even though we sought out different therapies and solutions, he continued to struggle. Most days, he would walk home from school, run into his bedroom, and slam the door behind him. In frustration, he often threw things around his room. Later, when he began playing the drums, he would retreat to his room and pound out his frustration.

I pleaded continually with the Lord to bring my son relief, to let him experience success. Yet Mark continued to struggle and didn't seem to have a sense of God's love for him even though he went to church and youth group.

One day when Mark was in high school, I felt helpless and hopeless. It was just too much. It had been going on too long. I'd cried so many tears over him and, this day, there didn't seem to be any help in sight. "Oh, Lord, please give him some success. Cause him to seek You, to see that You do love him and have a plan for him. You desire only his best, Lord, but sometimes I sure can't see it."

I don't know how it happened, but I unexpectedly felt as if I had been transported into heaven through a vision of what was to come. Surrounded by the glories of heaven, I was in awe. My tears stopped and I looked around stunned by its beauty and peace. A glint of light caught my attention and to my left I could see a round globe hanging in space. I realized, *That's the earth. Look how small it is. It looks so insignificant.* Simultaneously, I realized Mark's difficulties were on that small globe and I couldn't even see them. The earth appeared small and Mark's difficulties were even smaller.

That's how God views our problems, I realized. *They are very tiny to Him, yet so huge to us.* The enormity of our current problems can cause us to feel hopeless, but God isn't overwhelmed by them. Though our struggles are important to Him because He loves us, they are small in His eyes.

That glimmer of truth made my grief over Mark almost laughable. I realized with joy that God has no sense of hopelessness as I do. He knew exactly what He had in mind for Mark and He would fulfill it! I didn't need to be sad. Suddenly, I burst out laughing. It seemed so silly to be feeling helpless and hopeless when God already knew what He was going to do. I laughed, as my faith was once again restored.

That's what an eternal perspective and knowing we are future citizens of heaven can do for us. Once we transcend this earth and arrive in our heavenly destination, everything that was difficult here will be washed away with the joy of being in Jesus' presence.

Mark is now attending a Christian university and growing closer to God. Even though the final chapter of his struggles is not yet written, I know the Lord is in charge of his life and all of us as He views our earth from His heavenly vantage point.

Just Passing Through

Because we have a spiritual birth certificate and are headed for heaven, the thought of eternally living with Christ can make whatever we experience on this earth of minute importance. Second Corinthians 4:16-18 tells us the attitude we should have: "Therefore we do not lose heart, but though our outer man is decaying, yet our inner man is being renewed day by day. For momentary, light affliction is producing for us an eternal weight of glory far beyond all comparison, while we look not at the things which are seen, but at the things which are not seen; for the things which are seen are temporal, but the things which are not seen are eternal."

We're only passing through this earthly plane and there's a far better home waiting for us: no pain, no confusion, no struggle, no tears, no grief. Malcolm Muggeridge, a British journalist who spent most of his years battling Christianity, finally succumbed to Christ's wooing in his 70s. When he wrote the following, he's telling us about the heavenly viewpoint of knowing we have eternal life:

> I had a sense, sometimes enormously vivid, that I was a stranger in a strange land; a visitor, not a native . . . a displaced person . . . the feeling, I was surprised to find, gave me a great sense of satisfaction, almost of ecstasy. . . . Days or weeks or months might pass. Would it ever return—the lostness? I strained my ears to hear it, like distant music; my eyes to see it, a very bright light very far away. Has it gone forever? And then—ah! the relief. Like slipping away from a sleeping embrace, silently shutting a door behind one, tiptoeing off in the grey light of dawn—a stranger again. The only ultimate disaster that can befall us, I have come to realize, is to feel ourselves to be at home here on earth. As long as we are aliens, we cannot forget our true homeland.[2]

Are you seeking God's will for an important decision? Your spiritual birth certificate says you're entitled to God's wisdom. Do you feel discouraged because you can't get victory over a bad habit? Pray moment by moment for God's power. All these things that seem so hard are limited to that little earthly globe, and from heaven they look minuscule. God knows exactly what He's planning to do to help you.

If you and I will concentrate on our spiritual life, today's difficulties won't seem as hard. Someday, we're not going to struggle or suffer. We're bound for heaven and our spiritual birth certificate says we have eternal life.

Treasures in Heaven

Some of us have experienced the anticipation of having an opportunity to meet an important person or attend an event where an important person is participating or speaking. Maybe you've attended a conference where your favorite writer is speaking and you are looking forward to getting his or her autograph after you purchase the book. Several years ago, I felt excited about attending a political rally at election time and having the opportunity to personally see Elizabeth Dole. Although it was exciting, I felt a little let down that I could see her only from a distance and she didn't even know I was there.

I was encouraged to remember that in the future, you and I will attend an event that will feature the most famous Person in the world. His Book is the best-selling book of all time. He has been adored and appreciated by people on earth since He was born. Of course, you know I'm referring to Jesus. You and I will one day see Him face to face, and the greatest part is that He will know us personally! We won't be nameless faces in the crowd. He will call each of us by name and know the intimate details of our lives. And we will sense His incredible love and concern for us. Wouldn't we eagerly want to look forward to meeting Him, far more than any personality alive today?

Nothing on this earth can be compared to our eager waiting for the return of Jesus for His own children. Paul wrote, " . . .we eagerly wait for a Savior, the Lord Jesus Christ" (Philippians 3:20). The Greek word *apekdechometha* is translated "eagerly await" and suggests a "tiptoe" anticipation and longing. Although we may not be looking up into the sky every moment, in our hearts we can have

204 Transcendence

an anticipation of our future reunion with Jesus and an eternity of enjoying the blessings of heaven.

A few months ago, I thought I might be facing that as I flew in an airplane. No, they didn't announce that we were going to crash, but a cloud formation outside the plane's window appeared to me to be the entrance to heaven. As I've never seen before, beautiful white clouds formed a circle with blue sky as a backdrop. Leading up to the cloud circle were pastel-colored clouds looking like huge steps. It was the most beautiful thing I'd ever seen and I felt like Jacob looking at the staircase to heaven.

As I stared at the gorgeous sight, wishing I had a camera, I felt an intense desire to go to heaven. I wanted to run right out the wing of that airplane and walk toward that circle of light. Thinking of it right now makes me hunger for heaven because I know it will be even more wonderful than that—because my beloved Jesus will greet me beyond those clouds.

Author Joseph Stowell gives us an example of that kind of expectation in his book *Eternity*.

> My friend Bud Wood is the founder and developer of what has become one of the finest homes in America for mentally challenged children and adults. Shepherds Home, located in Union Grove, Wisconsin, ministers to many who are afflicted with Down's Syndrome. The staff at Shepherds makes a concentrated effort to present the gospel to these children. As a result many have understood and come to believe in Christ as Savior and in a heaven that will be their home.
>
> Bud once told me that one of the major maintenance problems they have at Shepherds is dirty windows.
>
> "What? How could that be a problem?" I asked.
>
> "You can walk through our corridors any time of the day," Bud explained, "and you will see some of these precious children standing with their hands, noses, and faces

pressed to the windows, looking up to see if Christ might
not be coming back right then to take them home and
make them whole."[3]

How many of us dirty our hearts' windows eagerly awaiting,
watching for, anticipating Christ's return? I must admit that at
times the puny attractions of this world dampen my enthusiasm
for joyful watching. I've heard my Christian friends and myself
joke, saying things like, "Oh, I hope Jesus doesn't come back until
I can experience married life . . . or have children . . . or complete
college. . . ." It's a natural tendency to want to experience all the
good things that this alien world can offer. I know I'd love to have
another one of my books on the best-seller list or enjoy a cruise
or see my daughter or son married. There are many things that
are very attractive. But once we reach heaven, we won't regret leaving any of it.

Perhaps Lot's wife was wrestling with this truth when she disobeyed the angel's command as he led her and her family out of
Sodom right before the destruction described in Genesis 19.
Maybe she had left behind a valuable antique of her mother's. Maybe
her best friend had been waving from her door as they scurried
down the road. What was so important that she disobeyed and, as
a result, sacrificed her life?

When I really stop to think of how much better heaven will
be, then anything this world offers is not even worthy of my con-
sideration. If God doesn't give me another best-seller before I die
or I don't go on a cruise, it won't matter once I'm in heaven. Whatever is so important to me right now from an earthly perspective
will have absolutely no value once I've arrived in my home town.
I will be walking on streets of gold!

J. Oswald Sanders, in his book, *Heaven, Better by Far,* sum-
marizes for us all the wonderful blessings we'll enjoy in God's
heavenly presence:

- We will bask in the immediate presence of the triune God.
- All that diminishes the quality of life on earth will be banished from heaven.
- The heights of joy we have experienced on earth will be eclipsed in heaven.
- We will be "saved to sin no more." Failure and its consequences will be a thing of the past.
- No more will we be subject to temptations from the world, the flesh, and the Devil.
- Knowledge will no longer be limited.
- Limitations of the body will hamper us no more.
- Everything that would enrich our lives will be available.
- Reunion with loved ones and the formation of new relationships will make heaven a wonderful place of fellowship.
- Heaven's music will far surpass earth's finest achievements in that realm.
- There will be full satisfaction for every holy and wholesome longing and aspiration.[4]

Hebrews 11:13-16 expresses an eternal perspective about those who have already died who had faith, but it also speaks to us: "All these died in faith, without receiving the promises, but having seen them and having welcomed them from a distance, and having confessed that they were strangers and exiles on the earth. For those who say such things make it clear that they're seeking a country of their own. And indeed if they had been thinking of that country from which they went out, they would have had opportunity to return. But as it is, they desire a better country, that is a heavenly one. Therefore God is not ashamed to be called their God; for He has prepared a city for them."

I'm convinced that when we step into that glorious city, leaving behind the pull of an earthly perspective, we'll say to Jesus the same thing the Queen of Sheba said to Solomon: "The half was not told me" (1 Kings 10:7). Even with all we know about heaven, I anticipate we have a very small view, don't you?

Having an eternal perspective keeps our focus on the complete satisfaction that heaven will offer. Such a perspective helps us to make our spiritual walk a priority. We'll be more interested in storing up our treasures in heaven than on earth. We'll give to missions with more passion. We'll see each unbelieving friend or family member with a desire to have them know Christ. We'll desire to live a righteous life because it will motivate others to join us in heaven.

Such truth reminds me of the far better place heaven will be. I want to turn over my heavenly passport so that I can be transported to a better world—my heavenly home.

Our Final Transformation

And why are we so excited, looking with great anticipation, fixing our eyes on the certainty of His return? Because we love His appearing and we're going to receive great benefits. We're going to be transformed into the perfection we've been craving all along! God will take the powdered dust of the saints long dead and fashion them again into their original likeness, but this time with spiritual bodies that will never die. In His amazing greatness, God will instantaneously change our flesh and blood bodies into bloodless, spiritual beings that will rise through the air and greet Him in the sky, transcending the pull of earth that formerly held us in bondage. We'll fly without wings. And I'm sure we'll simultaneously shout and sing our praises to such an awesome God!

For both those previously dead and those alive, we will instantaneously be transformed into "the body of His glory" (Philippians 3:21). We shall be "conformed to the image of His Son" (Romans 8:29) and "bear the image of the heavenly" (1 Corinthians 15:49). First John 3:2 tells us, "We know that, when He appears, we shall be like Him, because we shall see Him just as He is." First Corinthians 15:42-44 details that our bodies will be imperishable, glorious, powerful, and spiritual. In verse 53 of that chapter, we're told it will be "immortal."

Nothing can destroy it.

Nothing can harm it.

Nothing can make it feel pain or discomfort.

No wonder we can't wait!

Author John Foster expresses that in beautiful language when he writes, "Death is not, to the Christian, what it has often been called, 'Paying the debt of nature.' No, it is not paying a debt; it is rather like bringing a note to a bank to obtain solid gold in exchange for it. You bring a cumbrous body which is worth nothing, and which you could not wish to retain long; you lay it down, and receive for it, from the eternal treasures, liberty, victory, knowledge and rapture."[5]

The apostle Paul explains in Philippians 3:21 that this is possible through Jesus' "exertion of the power that He has even to subject all things to Himself." The words "power He has" comes from our word "dynamite." That's power! Dynamite can blow things apart and God's dynamic power can rearrange our molecules to become something supernatural and indestructible.

God's glorious plan for our final transformation increases our confidence in His ability to help us in our present struggles. If He can rearrange our molecules to give us an indestructible body, then He can help our child with Attention Deficit Disorder. If He can pull us away from earth's hold, He can cause our boss to show us favor if it's His will. If He can prepare a heavenly mansion, then He can bring a buyer for our house. All our earthly difficulties are no more difficult for God than our holding this book up to read it. Nothing is impossible for a God who has the end of the world already planned in minute detail and will fulfill each prophesy in His precise timing. Looking forward to our future transformation can increase our present faith. Our heavenly perspective can overshadow our earthly astigmatism. Everything that is happening to us is a part of God's plan and we can rejoice!

We are a strange people, aren't we? Citizens of heaven but called to do kingdom work on this distant planet. A. W. Tozer says it best when he writes, "A real Christian is an odd number anyway. He feels supreme love for One whom he has never seen, talks familiarly every day to Someone he cannot see, expects to go to heaven on the virtue of Another, empties himself in order to be full, admits he is wrong so he can be declared right, goes down in order to get up, is strongest when he is weakest, richest when he is poorest, and happiest when he feels worst. He dies so he can live, forsakes in order to have, gives away so he can keep, sees the invisible, hears the inaudible, and knows that which passeth knowledge."[6]

It's just like wearing wool clothing on a hot day when you anticipate flying to a cold climate. When you're wearing your heavenly citizen's clothes and carrying your heavenly passport, you may be considered foolish walking through the airport waiting for your plane to depart. But once you arrive at your destination, you'll be dressed for eternity, drenched in glory, and overflowing with praise!

Is your nose pressed against this window of earth, looking eagerly for your deliverance from earth's difficulties? Someday you'll be called home, but until then, live here as a citizen of heaven, rejoicing in the benefits your heavenly birth certificate provides and anticipating your final transformation.

❧ *Questions* ❧

1. Review Philippians 3:20-21. When you think of a "citizen of heaven," what do you think should characterize such a person? To what degree do you believe you live as such a person?

2. In what aspect of your life do you want to live out your "alien status" more actively?

3. As you strive to live as a "kingdom child," how does 2 Corinthians 4:13-18:

   ▪ encourage you?

   ▪ instruct you?

   ▪ give you God's perspective?

4. Review Hebrews 11:13-16. How do those verses encourage you and give you hope?

5. Consider the list of the blessings of being in heaven detailed by J. Oswald Sanders on page 206. Which of those is most important to you? How does it relate to a difficulty you're facing right now?

6. Now that you have given more thought to the differences between an earthly and an eternal perspective, consider the story I told of the ducks at the beginning of chapter 1. In what way are you like those ducks, wanting to do what you think is best, though God seems to indicate otherwise?

7. Now review the chart on page 15. Which earthly perspectives do you tend to adopt most often? Which eternal perspectives have you most made your own?

8. What reactions do you see resulting from living with earthly perspectives? Think of an example of how an earthly viewpoint influenced your thinking or reacting even within the past week.

9. In light of what you've learned about seeing through God's eyes, what would you do differently now if you could turn back the clock?

10. Read 2 Kings 6:8-17. Can you identify with the servant's fear in regard to some circumstances you're facing right now? How will seeing your situation through God's eyes help you to trust God's plan, now and for eternity?

11. What do you look forward to the most as you think of being transformed when Jesus returns?

Notes

Chapter Two — *Grace*

1. Philip Yancey, "What's So Amazing About Grace," *Christianity Today*, October 6, 1997, p. 52.
2. Kay Arthur, based on her testimony in *Lord, I Want to Know You* (Portland, OR: Multnomah, 1992), p. 44.

Chapter Three — *Identity*

1. John Ortberg, "What's Really Behind Our Fatigue," *Leadership Journal*, Spring 1997, p.108.
2. Marjorie Miller, "Spring Cleaning Not Just a Chore as Israeli Women Ready for Holiday," *Los Angeles Times*, April 18, 1997, p. A18.
3. Miller, p. A18.
4. Herbert Lockyer, *All the Women of the Bible* (Grand Rapids, MI: Zondervan).
5. Charles Swindoll, *Laugh Again* (Dallas, TX: Word, 1991), p. 57. Used by permission.
6. Donna Goodrich, in my book *God's Vitamin C for the Spirit of Women* (Lancaster, PA: Starburst, 1996), p. 281.

Chapter Four —*Faith*

1. Charles Stanley, in a letter sent out September 1998, to ministry friends through InTouch Ministries.
2. Stanley letter.
3. Jennifer Maze Brown, "Empty Arms," *Today's Christian Woman*, May/June 1998, p. 42.
4. Brown, p. 42.

Chapter Five — *Purpose*

1. Kay Arthur, *Lord, I Want To Know You* (Portland, OR: Multnomah, 1992), p. 23.
2. Kenneth S. Wuest, *Philippians in the Greek New Testament* (Grand Rapids, MI: Eerdmans, 1942), p. 44.

3. Warren W. Wiersbe, *Be Joyful* (Wheaton, IL: Victor, 1974), pp. 37-38. Used by permission.

Chapter Six — *Service*
1. Joseph Stowell, *Eternity* (Chicago: Moody Press, 1995), p. 58. Used by permission.
2. Jean Fleming, *Between Walden and the Whirlwind* (Colorado Springs, CO: NavPress, 1985), p. 43.

Chapter Seven—*Humility*
1. Thomas Fuller, quoted in *Topical Encyclopedia of Living Quotations* (Minneapolis: Bethany, 1982), p. 66.
2. Matthew A. Castille, as quoted in *Topical Encyclopedia of Living Quotations* (Minneapolis: Bethany, 1982), p. 66.
3. Joseph Stowell, *Eternity* (Chicago: Moody Press, 1995), p. 144.
4. Herbert Lockyer, *All the Women of the Bible* (Grand Rapids, MI: Zondervan), p. 87.
5. Warren W. Wiersbe, *Be Joyful* (Wheaton, IL: Victor Books, 1974), p. 50. Used by permission.
6. Richard Foster, "Becoming Like Christ," *Christianity Today*, February 5, 1996.
7. Gene Getz, *A Profile of Christian Maturity* (Grand Rapids, MI: Zondervan, 1976), p. 108.
8. Tony Evans, *Returning to Your First Love* (Chicago: Moody Press, 1995), p. 183.
9. Richard B. Douglass, "Quotable Quotations," *Christianity Today*, Volume 31, p. 17.

Chapter Eight —*Forgiveness*
1. Kevin Downing, Ph.D., and Peter Robbins, Ph.D., in a pamphlet called *Beyond Bitterness* (Turning Point Ministries, 1993), p. 3.
2. Warren W. Wiersbe, *Be Joyful* (Wheaton, IL: Victor Books, 1974), p. 98. Used by permission.
3. Wiersbe, p. 99.
4. Barbara Johnson, *Mama, Get the Hammer! There's a Fly on Papa's Head* (Dallas: Word, 1994), p. 36.
5. Doug Manning, *Don't Take My Grief Away* (San Francisco: HarperSanFrancisco, 1984).
6. Marilyn Willett Heavilin, *I'm Listening, Lord* (Nashville, TN: Nelson).
7. Charles Swindoll, *Laugh Again* (Dallas: Word, 1991), p. 148. Used by permission.
8. Wiersbe, p. 93.
9. William Hendricksen, *New Testament Commentary, Exposition of Philippians* (Grand Rapids, MI: Baker Book House, 1962), p. 173.

Chapter Nine — *Surrender*
1. Arlene Kaiser, from my book *God's Abundance* (Lancaster, PA: Starburst, 1997), November 18.
2. Lloyd John Ogilvie, *Let God Love You* (Waco, TX: Word, 1974), p. 82.
3. John F. Walvoord, *Philippians, Triumph in Christ* (Chicago: Moody Press, 1971), p. 65.

Chapter Ten — *Contentment*
1. A. W. Tozer, *The Pursuit of God* (Harrisburgh, PA: Christian Publications, 1982).
2. William Barclay, *The Letters to the Philippians, Colossians, and Thessalonians, Revised Edition* (Louisville, KY: Westminster, 1975), p. 85.
3. Charles Swindoll, *Laugh Again* (Dallas: Word, 1991), p. 200. Used by permission.
4. Lloyd John Ogilvie, *Let God Love You* (Waco, TX: Word, 1974), p. 142.
5. Kenneth S. Wuest, *Philippians in the Greek New Testament* (Grand Rapids, MI: Wm. B. Eerdmans, 1942).
6. Swindoll, p. 51.
7. Barclay, p. 79.
8. John Archer, "Can America Do the Right Thing?," *Aspire*, Feb./March 1995.
9. Barclay, p. 80.
10. Larry J. Crabb, Jr., *Effective Biblical Counseling* (Grand Rapids, MI: Zondervan, 1977), p. 114.
11. Crabb, p. 116.

Chapter Eleven — *Transcendence*
1. Joseph M. Stowell, *Eternity* (Chicago: Moody Press, 1995), p. 110. Used by permission.
2. Malcolm Muggeridge, *Jesus Rediscovered* (New York: Doubleday, 1979), pp. 47-48, as quoted in Joni Eareckson Tada, *Heaven, Your Real Home* (Grand Rapids, MI: Zondervan, 1995), pp. 96-97.
3. Stowell, p. 122.
4. J. Oswald Sanders, *Heaven, Better by Far* (Grand Rapids, MI: Discovery House Radio Bible Class, 1993), pp. 22-23.
5. John Foster, as quoted in Harold Ivan Smith's *Once in a Lifetime* (Nashville, TN: Thomas Nelson, 1998), p. 75.
6. A. W. Tozer, *The Root of Righteousness* (Camp Hill, PA: Christian Publications, 1955), p. 156.

About the Author

KATHY COLLARD MILLER is God's daughter, Larry's wife, Darcy and Mark's mom, and an author of more than forty books, including *God's Abundance, When Counting to Ten Isn't Enough*, and the best-selling *God's Vitamin C for the Spirit*.

As a speaker who shares God's love with audiences across the United States and into foreign countries, Kathy's desire is that women embrace their incredible inheritance in Christ and consider themselves precious because they are princesses of the King of kings. Audiences around the world have enjoyed Kathy's presentations, which include humor, vulnerable sharing, and practical, biblical insights.

Kathy is a graduate of C.L.A.S.S. (Christian Leaders, Authors, Speakers Seminar) and is on the teaching staff of that seminar, which is taught by Florence Littauer and Marita Littauer. She is also a member of the National Speakers Association (NSA).

Kathy has appeared extensively on television and radio programs, including the *700 Club, 100 Huntley Street, Moody Radio*, and many others.

Kathy and her husband live in Placentia, California. She can be reached for speaking engagements at P. O. Box 1058, Placentia, CA, 92871 or Kathyspeak@aol.com.

For information about CLASSeminars and their products, or to book Kathy, or over 150 other speakers, call (800) 433-6633.